ON A RANT FROM WA1

ON A RANT FROM WATFORD TO CHIRK

A JOURNEY BY NARROWBOAT

MARTIN FARMER

YOUCAXTON PUBLICATIONS
OXFORD & SHREWSBURY

YouCaxton Publications
enquiries@youcaxton.co.uk

To all the wonderful people encounterd during this adventure

Simon and Linda thank you for your invaluable help and support during the voyage and beyond.

To all the others that annoyed and irritated me for three weeks... you are forgiven.

Martin Farmer a classically trained chef and former soldier. Martin served for twelve years in the Regular Army. Stationed in Germany and UK, he also completed two active service tours of Northern Ireland during the conflict in the province. After a sabbatical of eight years he joined the Territorial Army. This time diversifying and became an instructor in the equally 'dark arts' of Physical Training and Nuclear Biological and Chemical defence.

In civilian life Martin worked as a chef at The Royal Masonic School for Girls in Rickmansworth Hertfordshire.

A life long interest in physical fitness Martin dabbled in the triathlon scene for a few years during the sports formative years in the UK. This led to many years of competitive running and cycle racing at club level, both on and off road.

Having relocated to North Wales, Martin now spends his days awaiting official retirement participating in several pursuits. Most of his summer months are spent with his friend and colleague Simon. Together they travel to various parts of the country to teach bush craft skills and deliver talks and presentations on World War One.

Martins other passions are performing magic, walking, the occasional fly fishing trip and oil painting.

Preface

I first met Martin well over thirty years ago when we served together in the Armed Forces. Our common bond was as that of soldiers and our mutual love of exercise and the countryside. One week during our annual leave, Martin came to stay at my sister's farm and we walked and ran the Malvern Hills and other beautiful areas of Hereford and Worcestershire. As is often the case in the military, we lost contact for twenty-five years (the advantages of modern technology).

A typical Yorkshireman with a dry, dour sense of humour allied to keeping his pennies in his pocket when he can, Martin has an easy-going nature but underneath the surface a steely resolve. In years gone by, he was a cyclist of some note and was one of the oldest soldiers to have passed the Army's course to become a Physical Training Instructor.

He would need these traits for his journey to relocate by narrowboat from Watford to Chirk, virtually single handed, not an undertaking I would like to try on my own!

I remember him a few years ago talking about his love of the Llangollen area and how he liked the place, along with distant memories of pretty Welsh maidens.

Once he started his journey, it was good to track him coming to "God's Country", speaking to him by phone or email every forty-eight hours or so, dependant on the signal. It was also interesting to see his mood change depending on how many locks each day, duration of time at the helm and his brushes with other boat users!

During his last week, my wife Linda and I joined him for about five days, by which time, he was certainly looking forward to "Docking" in at Chirk but with the extra help reducing the pressure, Martin gradually seemed to start enjoying the scenery once on the "Shroppie" and Llangollen Canals.

And now, eighteen-plus months ahead, here we are. He has put pen to paper and I am sure his "Journey" of many kinds will make an interesting read to narrow boat users and readers in general.

Simon Jarman MBE

Introduction

I have never been a very ambitious person, although when I think about my sixty odd years, I have probably done a great deal more things than the average person. I do feel quite proud of the fact that now and then I have given myself definite goals to reach and when these pinnacles have been attained, the feeling of satisfaction cannot be bettered. This book is about one such goal.

This is the story of a quite ambitious journey by boat, most of it tackled alone. It took place over a three-week period in the summer of 2015. The whole thing was seemingly sustained on a diet of luxury ice creams. This was the monumental summer when we had no fewer than five dry days! The route was from Watford in Hertfordshire, via one or two metaphorical detours to Chirk near Wrexham, which used to be just a town but has now morphed into an entire a county. -

If you the reader, are expecting me to get all enthusiastic talking about boatman's cabins and hand-painted coalscuttles adorned with the inevitable roses and castles, you might like to spend your money on something else. Likewise, those easily offended may be disturbed to find a complete lack of reference to political correctness. There are also one or two adult words within these pages but absolutely nothing that you would not hear on any BBC program shown after nine pm.

If I speak unfavourably about a person (and there are a few of those) and you think the person described could be you, then please be assured that this story is a complete work of fiction and any resemblance to you is pure coincidence (although some say there is no such thing). On the other hand, if I lavish praise on someone and again, you think it could be you, be assured that every word that I have written is the absolute truth!

During this journey, I kept a fairly detailed diary of each day's events. However sometimes, due to the pressure of steering, navigating and drinking tea some occasional details may have become blurred. Therefore, when I describe a location or scene, my recollections may be somewhat different to those of other boaters: I have only written about what I believe I saw. So, if I say a certain lock was fourteen feet wide it may well have been really fifteen and a half feet etc. (And yes, I do know that canals are not really three inches deep!)

The Start

I had a new job, and found myself exiled once again to the South East of England. I say once again, because I had an unfortunate knack of ending up down there, I didn't want to go – but work is work. I had served in the Regular Army and much of this time had been spent in the south, in between trips to a few other places. Even after leaving the service, this trend continued; I was a chef, and this latest employment would see me working and living in a private school for almost the next seventeen years

There was a documentary on the television a few years ago, commemorating the 1984 miners' strike, a police officer explained how, during the year-long dispute, he, along with many other officers from the Metropolitan Police, had to spend week after week in the 'Peoples Republic of South Yorkshire' (I really saw this title written on a road side sign once). He said that the only thing that kept him motivated was knowing that he would be able to return, every Friday afternoon to his preferred utopia in Hackney, Hayes or wherever he came from – presumably the strikers didn't do picket lines at weekends. I had been employed briefly in the mining industry for around eighteen months, before deciding to take the oath and join the army. I have always felt hugely relieved that I wasn't involved in the dispute, which was for so many, an awful and harrowing episode in their lives

But I could empathise with this policeman; I owned a house in the very heartland of the area that had caused his anguish. Originally I briefly considered commuting back and forth but realised that three hours on the M1 each way before and after a nine-hour shift was not very practical. So, for several years I accepted the situation: the job and the salary were agreeable and the generous school holidays with pay were also welcome. At first, just like the policeman, I couldn't wait to get home at every opportunity but over the next few years, I gradually moved various bits and pieces of my creature comforts down to the home counties.

This all seemed to happen without any conscious effort on my part, until it slowly dawned on me that my flat at the school had become my home and my house in Yorkshire was becoming less and less welcoming on each return trip. For years I had been involved in competitive cycling and running and I had become well acquainted with most of the back lanes and roads of Herts, Bucks and Beds. Although not quite a match for the rugged splendour of the Yorkshire Dales, I had developed some fondness for the Chiltern hills

I had a good social life, had made friends and in fact things felt quite rosy. A strange metamorphosis had taken place and I had actually come to like living in the south. Even London I decided, was quite an exciting place and conversely, I didn't particularly like going home to Yorkshire anymore – not the bit that I belonged to anyway.

So, after two break-ins in the space of a week and the appearance of some delightful neighbours from Hell, I eventually made the decision to sell my property,

Time passed, personalities came and went; the work got harder and the holidays became shorter.

More alarming was that my free accommodation was to come to an end, meaning I would eventually lose over half of my wages in rent. Most worrying of all, I had openly criticised my manager on several occasions and he was now determined to single me out at every opportunity and make an example of me.

I had briefly looked at the possibility of buying a narrowboat about ten years previously, then got cold feet, deciding that my predicament was not so bad, so I plodded on, becoming more and more unhappy. I was now stuck in a job that I hated, becoming increasingly institutionalised and with the average south eastern property rent higher than my monthly salary; I was feeling as trapped as an England football manager in a room full of journalists.

I came across an article one day saying that due to the recent events in the banking world, our savings, if we had any, were worth almost nothing interest-wise. It went on to suggest that buying a narrowboat would be a good investment. Granted, this was an article about boats and not finance so the author was, I suspected, a tad biased – but it got me thinking again.

Television was becoming less and less appealing, with the constant stream of *Britain's Got Sheep* or *Let's Destroy Some Poor Bugger's Self Esteem Tonight.* I preferred to while away my hours watching conspiracy theory programmes on *YouTube* encouraging us not to be 'sheeple' or that the mystery planet X or Nibiru, was going to collide with us in the near future. You may snigger but the Russians claim to know a lot about this threat – obviously this has still to come to pass at the time of writing – are you reading this David Icke!

Whatever the future held, I decided that buying a boat could be a good move. Affordable and hopefully safe from the anarchists and looters. These probably would be more concerned that they could no longer log onto their *Facebook* accounts, rather than the probability of massive food shortages for those who survived the forthcoming apocalypse.

I told one of the school gardeners about my plan and she said that her partner had a boat he wanted to sell and most importantly, it came with a mooring on a marina. That term always seemed strange – to me marina means maritime, or pertaining to the sea – while the Grand Union Canal and most others in this country are I think, at least fifty miles inland. Still it must be correct because I noted just the other day whilst looking at a map, that *The Ordnance Survey* uses the convention on their wonderful maps...and the *OS* are always right!

After looking at the boat with someone who knew them better than I did and after heeding the warning, 'don't expect a luxury yacht for that price' I did not ask for luxury, nor did I get it. It was a *Springer,* one of Market Harbough's finest vessels. Sam Springer's boats have a dubious reputation amongst most boaty people in the know, although to be fair to the long-gone Sam, some people will not hear a bad word said about these craft. The usual argument was that they were all built from British steel, as opposed to that foreign rubbish we are now afflicted with (I understand that one can now buy a Chinese-built narrow boat! I wonder how long it takes to deliver one?). I was now on a steep learning curve regarding boats and having read one or two horror stories about these Leicestershire vessels, I was beginning to sweat, wondering if I had made a monumental mistake – again.

The vendor informed me that the boat's current mooring could not be taken for granted and I would have to undergo the scrutiny of Frank, the marina manager. So, one afternoon after work, I went off to meet him. I suspect that Frank had originally come from the East End but I managed to give a good account of myself and he finally agreed, after explaining all the rules (there were lots). The most important of these was that dogs would not be tolerated but that I could indeed tie my newly acquired purchase to one of his scaffolding and wood jetties in exchange for quite a lot of money.

I subsequently learned that Frank ran the place with the relaxed and nonchalant air of a Regimental Sergeant Major tasked with rehearsing the Trooping of the Colour. Although mainly confined to a mobility scooter after some road traffic accident, he would occasionally spring up from it like a riled cobra head, butting anyone he deemed to be particularly obnoxious. One potential customer had barely emerged from his *BMW* before Frank attacked him and he once tore into me, thankfully only verbally, because he suspected I had splashed water on to the tiles surrounding the communal shower. He forgave me eventually though and we became quite matey. Bark worse than bite I suppose... unless you drove a German car.

By now it was the summer holidays and I was spending most days with a *Black and Decker* drill and sanding disk, grinding patches of rust and old faded paint off the superstructure with the intention of repainting her. The good old British weather was cooperating by turning scorching hot most days, making work unbearable after around two each afternoon and I was becoming increasingly concerned about the serviceability of my new toy, so I made the decision that I would have to have the boat taken out of the water and blackened. If you are now thinking surely, he must have had a survey done, well no I did not. It is a long story and this book is supposed to be about my epic voyage, so I will get to that in good time and spare you the details about my naivety.

There was a boat repair yard adjacent to the marina but the two clowns who owned it being notorious for being rather difficult. One of them bore more than a passing resemblance to Basil Fawlty, both in appearance and manner, though he was much more menacing. As I approached, 'Basil' was up a ladder melting holes in the side of a boat with an oxygen acetylene torch. Removing his visor, his eyes locked onto me like lasers, so that for a moment I was concerned I was about to become a symbiotic part of a boat. Thankfully he turned the torch off and came down the ladder to demand the reason for my intrusion. When we got into the office, his mate, a 'Smirf'-like character, came over to join in the fun and they both spent the next fifteen minutes or so, explaining to me with great delight, exactly why *Springers* were so bad. (If any Springer owner reading this is thinking litigation, this was their opinion, and is not necessarily mine). Their main gripe was that, unlike almost all other narrow boats, *Springers* have 'v'-shaped hulls rather than the more common flat ones. The reason for flat bottoms is because most canals, as I would discover later, are on average about three inches deep!

This unusual *Springer* design quirk they told me, can cause condensation to accumulate in the bottom so that even if the hull were sound below the water line, my boat would probably rot from the inside out (boats are painted below the water line with thick black sticky bitumen every few years to stop the hull rusting away). Finally, they agreed to have a look at her and to re-black the hull – for a fee that made my eyes water. At the same time, they warned me that when they pressure-hosed it, there was a distinct possibility that they could puncture the hull, due to the turkey foil-like thinness of the steel plating that old Sam had normally used. I didn't sleep too well that night, knowing that I had likely bought something with the aquatic equivalent of Dutch elm disease.

I later read that there really is such an affliction as 'boat pox' – apparently, they can catch measles too!

It turned out that things were not quite as bad as their gloomy predictions and the hull was in quite good nick, which was just as well, because by now I had managed to get right under the skin of the HR woman at work. In December 2013, things came to a head and I left by mutual agreement with a few quid extra in my bank account – and moved onto the boat permanently – well for about a year.

My mate Tom the school caretaker, was a veritable fount of wisdom regarding most things that float. That's what he said anyway and he should know, because he told me once about how he had almost succeeded in blowing himself to bits during a trip on the Thames – something to do with petrol, alcohol and a running generator. Tom did know quite a lot about boating though, certainly more than me – but there again, most of Year Three at the school knew more than I did.

Tom took me out on a few occasions during the previous summer and autumn, so that I could get the hang of things. However, on our first outing, neither of us thought to check on how much fuel we had, or not. When the penny finally dropped, we were quite relieved to get back without having to do a shire horse impersonation, pulling a dead fifty-five-foot boat home. Another voyage in October found us miles away from Watford at a rather pleasant canal-side pub and Tom had just ordered his third pint when he commented to me that it was now four o'clock-ish. I pointed out that it had taken us four hours to get here and because it was October, things got dark around six. Somehow, we managed to find our way back, with the last two hours in total darkness – funny how you always think that you are moving faster in the dark – apparently, the average tube train goes at about twenty miles per hour, seems much faster in a dark tunnel though.

After a few more of these little adventures, it was becoming increasingly obvious to me that I did not really much like messing about in boats: I found it quite tedious once the novelty of seeing familiar places from a different perspective wore off – like the bottom of my boat, my enthusiasm was wearing a bit thin. This was probably down to my personality type, although I do not have the slightest problem with bone idleness on my own terms. This was just all too pedestrian for my liking; remember, this project was for one reason only…somewhere to lay my head.

Initially the plan was to renovate the boat, which frankly was in a bit of a mess when I bought it. But another year had passed by and I had not yet managed to do anything of real substance. Tom had promised to help me with the necessary work that was required, and to his credit, he did do a lot to help me adjust to living on the water.

What neither of us knew at the time was that he was about to be incapacitated with a serious heart defect which would understandably put him out of action for some time. Also, I had been suffering from carpal tunnel syndrome for a number of years (a common ailment in the catering industry) and I had already one hand mended, only for the problem to reappear in the other one but far worse this time. The pain was excruciating and I spent night after night without any proper sleep – something that I would not wish on my worst enemies – well maybe a few of them. This re-occurrence was caused mainly by doing various tasks on the boat, one of which was removing hundreds of rusted screws from the floor so that I could inspect the steel work for signs of the dreaded corrosion that my friends across the marina had predicted.

There are some good aspects of social media after all and over the past year or so, I had become reacquainted with Simon, an old army friend, with whom I had served over thirty years before. Simon now lived in Shropshire and he kindly invited me to come and visit him; so off I went, to an area I had not seen since I was only three feet tall. Then it was just a glimpse, as we passed through England's largest inland county on our way to the annual family pilgrimage to Pembrokeshire

I paid a second visit to Shropshire the following year, between Christmas and New Year. Simon too, had now bought a narrowboat which was moored at Chirk Marina, just over the border in Wales and on New Year's Day he took me to have a look at it. Unlike my investment, this vessel looked and felt the part. I casually asked Simon how much he was paying for his 330 square feet of water and when he answered, I realised it was considerably less than I was paying for a similar sized area in Watford. This should have been no surprise; I was after all, paying for the privilege of living in the south east. Now that I was unemployed, there was no longer any point dwelling in the world's most expensive region apart from Japan

Apart from my sports and physical pursuits, I was also a reasonably good close-up magician, doing occasional events, such as weddings, birthday parties etc. Now, my interest had turned specifically to street performing and busking (or as someone better than me once said, professional begging!). After dabbling with it for a few years in Watford, St Albans (and once on the South Bank (where the Brazilian security guard at least had the decency to wait for me to finish the trick that I was doing, before telling me it was private property and I couldn't perform there.... Oh well, nothing ventured). I had discovered that I could actually make some money at it – which got me thinking – I already knew that North Wales and Shropshire were attractive to tourists from all over the world (I shouldn't mention Shropshire really because it is a bit of a secret; we don't want every Tom, Dick and Harry flocking here) and I reckoned that if I could busk successfully in Watford town centre, which is full mainly with busy office workers and shoppers – then it could also work in a more relaxed tourist-dense area.

So, the decision was made: I was going to move, not necessarily to Chirk but away from Watford and the home counties. My only major problem was that I would need to get rid of *Sea Goat*, which I knew without doubt, would not get me much beyond Hunton Bridge, about an hour's walk from Watford, let alone a third of the way up the country. On all our previous voyages, the engine tended to overheat, not to mention the constant intake of water into the bilge. This was despite paying '*Basil Fawlty*' and his mate a small fortune to fix things but there you are, 'a fool and his money'.

Soon after returning to Hertfordshire, I was having one of those chance conversations with another, somewhat more scrupled marine engineer, Ralph. I had great faith in Ralph because he once got my engine started by spraying it with a damp start aerosol when it was being particularly obstinate and refusing to fire and when I mentioned payment, he looked at me as if I had propositioned borrowing his wife for an hour or so. I quickly put the wallet back in my pocket and sincerely thanked him; he then warned me never to try this myself because this spray was like heroin to a diesel engine. I stood there with my mouth open and said, 'really', wondering if there was such a thing as diesel methadone. I think I know a few people who could possibly be taking it.

On this occasion, I commented that I would like to get rid of *Sea Goat*. Ralph asked me how much I wanted for her and I named a figure sufficient to cover what I had spent on her; he said give me five minutes and vanished. The five minutes passed and instead of Ralph coming back, a quite elderly man appeared, who looked as if he had spent most of his life bare knuckle fighting on a fairground. He introduced himself but his name completely escapes me now, I'll make one up if I mention him later! He came straight to the point asking if I really wanted to sell the boat and then offered me exactly the price that I wanted.

Sticking out a shovel-sized hand, he said with some menace; 'If we shake on it there is no changing your mind, you know,' thus confirming that he was from a fairground'.

I readily shook, and couldn't quite believe that I had got rid of it so easily. He probably couldn't believe his luck either – I found out later that he sold it on for almost double the amount he had paid me. When I heard about this, I just thought there was no point in getting my knickers in a twist, so I just let the elastic get a bit tighter. After all, I had got my dosh back and obviously he would be looking at making a mark-up. Come on though, double? He could have a least done some work on it first. I knew about this because I would go over and have a discrete nosey every few days when no one was watching. I suppose at least it is nice knowing there are even more gullible people than me out there.

We discussed a time period, a completion date I suppose; he mentioned there wasn't any hurry because he had a few other boats to sort out and an up-and-coming boxing match on Croxley Green. (That last bit isn't actually true but it wouldn't have surprised me), We agreed on the end of March; it was mid-February now and unseasonably warm and sunny. I had several weeks to find something better and then I could put my plan into action

The only regret that I had about seeing the last of *Sea Goat* was (you don't really believe that was her name, do you?) that I had recently installed a wonderful multi-fuel stove to replace the somewhat dodgy diesel burner. The previous owner between sips of whiskey at eleven one morning had insisted that this thing ran on petrol and he was certain the diesel engine did too.

My decision to upgrade was due to my next-door neighbour who was a police officer and just like all plods, knew lots of 'interesting' people. One of these, Pete, owned a small forest, and kindly agreed to let us have as much wood as our hearts desired. It was a terrifying experience going to collect the wood from Pete's smallholding, where he lived with his wife, six ginger haired kids and a couple of man-eating wolves. He was around five feet tall and about the same across the shoulders and he wore a tee shirt adorned with the catchy slogan, 'Doing it the Sligo Way.' I wondered what the Sligo way was and suspected that he too may have originated from the travelling fraternity. Most of Pete's conversation was about fighting, including the latest victims of the dogs, one of which eyed me with suspicion constantly. We only ever got one consignment of wood because the kindly gentleman had, whilst presumably doing it 'The Sligo Way', poleaxed himself with one of his own trees: I do not know if he survived, or not.

Just like I have always done with most major issues throughout my life, I let things slide for ages until, around the second week in March I realised it might be a good idea to pull my finger out and luckily, I found a nice-looking boat at the right price almost immediately when I logged on to '*Apollo Duck*'. It was on the river Ure at Boroughbridge, in Yorkshire. I drove straight up there the next day, picking my dad up on the way, thinking he would enjoy the day out. Sadly, it would prove to be one of his last.

When we got to Boroughbridge, it was quite a few degrees colder than 'darn sarf' – some things never change. However, we looked at the boat and it was just as good as the photos suggested. However, it turned out that there was no mooring for it as they were quite scarce in that area. Also, boaters tend to keep things close to their chests.

Over the next two days, I drove around 500 miles, looking at marinas and boats to no avail. I saw a likely looking vessel at Sowerby Bridge, of '*Happy Valley*' fame, sitting right in the heart of the Pennines and offered to buy it but the couple selling the boat on behalf of the owners obviously did not much like the look of me and sold it to someone else: maybe they thought I was dodgy. It was all very peculiar because I had offered the full asking price and really couldn't do much more. In the event, their selling the boat to someone less suspicious did me a huge favour because as you will probably recall, lots of Yorkshire was inundated with severe floods last Christmas.

Returning to Watford empty handed, I relayed my fruitless efforts to my law enforcement neighbours Stan, the more effeminate of the two, reminded me that Sheila, who was moored nearby, was still selling her boat *Salamander*, after the previous potential buyer had got cold feet, being worried that because she was a bit on the large size, she might get stuck in one of the narrower parts of the vessel. Sheila was maybe in her sixties and had, by all accounts, had enough of boat dwelling. She had found a flat through the Three Rivers Council and had already moved out from the boat, so it took a couple of days for me to get hold of her to express my interest.

There was no name written on the side of the boat but rather unusually, the triangle-shaped glass at the front or bow in the cratch, was engraved with a rather good impression of a lizard, with the name *Salamander* tattooed below it. This was surrounded by a fancy pattern, also etched into the glass. This art work served two purposes; apart from identifying the boat, it also cleared up any confusion just in case anyone was not quite sure what a salamander was. I assumed that real Salamanders were emerald green because that was the colour the boat was (quite badly) painted. It was only while doing some Google research with the intention of re painting her that I discovered they are no such thing; black and yellow are more typical, although some also had red bits and pieces, just to make them look more interesting.

During my early days training to be a chef, French culinary terms were much in vogue and we were always admonished (for well, anything really) – particularly when we lost concentration for a second in the heat of battle and mistakenly called the flaming hot thing where one cooked bacon, fish, steaks or toast – a grill. "It's not a grill, it's a f-ing salamander!" our scary mentors would shout at us. It's been a grill for most of my life until now, I always thought and for the best part of forty years I have scratched my head, wondering why the French would name a grill after a lizard.

But there again, why call chips 'apples of the earth fried'? I blame the Absinthe. Interestingly, anyone in the real culinary world who used the amphibian word was considered to be a pretentious 'dick head'- and there aren't many of those in the catering industry! Did someone say 'pan fried?' – I always found an umbrella was a much more suitable implement to cook chicken breasts in!

Sheila knew about the same amount regarding her boat as I did about crocheting – nothing! In the entire time she had lived on the boat, the engine had never run and she was amazed when I got it going in seconds by turning on the battery isolators. We couldn't determine who the builders had been, despite all the relevant paper work that had accumulated in a box file for years on end.

Talking to other people in the know, they thought that *Salamander* was a mongrel – two different boats stuck together – try as I did I could never find the join. Apparently, this is quite a common occurrence – not hidden joints but stretched boats. She was created in the 1970s, so was even older than the *Sea Goat* I had just got rid of and although Sheila originally wanted more than I could afford, she agreed to drop the amount by two grand. Frank had already tipped me the wink about this and talking to him and Ralph – and anyone else who felt like joining in – the consensus was that it was a decent boat, although in need of a refit. So, I bought her and at the time of writing this, she is still floating.

I traipsed back and forth between boats for a week or so, moving my possessions and at the same time dumping anything that was not vital. I had already done this only a year or so earlier when I moved onto the first boat, only to find that I had accumulated a million more bits and pieces. I spent an interesting couple of days rooting through the engine room and other hiding places discovering all the bits and bobs that Sheila had left me and were included in the sale of the boat. These are some of them but the list isn't exhaustive:

Six miniature dustbins.

Eight tins of various types of paint -mostly emerald green.

Four coal shovels.

Three fire-side companions.

Two eco-fans.

Five baskets of clothes pegs.

Three giant paper butterflies.

One massive bundle of wire wool.

One unused barbecue grill.

One almost new generator.

Three power cables.

Two grappling hooks.

Two lump hammers.
Dozens of twelve-volt power adaptors.
One catapult.
Four windlasses.
Two tiny porcelain cats.
Three tins of Brasso.

There was also enough bedding to keep most of the 'Calais Jungle' residents warm all winter and I was very grateful for all of it. You can't buy catapults anywhere these days you know!

My thoughts turned now to making the move to pastures new; I wasn't really sure if it was feasible to travel hundreds of miles by narrowboat, especially single-handed.

I know that the canal system was created to transport goods over long distance, but they had horses to do the hauling and horses didn't break down like a diesel engine might. I suppose they did occasionally topple over through sheer exhaustion and boredom, in which case, they probably just rolled them into the cut along with everything else and stole another horse from the nearest field.

I made a few enquiries amongst the experts in the marina but they all agreed that it would be no problem, reassuring me to just take my time and don't rush things. When they asked how long I intended to take to get to North Wales, where I had decided I was definitely heading, I said about a month. A few people were adamant that 200-plus miles could be covered in something like four days to a week – at an average speed of one mile per hour? It just didn't equate; each time I would say; 'What's that in then, a Royal Marines rigid raider?' I always got the same reply but with a bit less conviction; 'No, no mate, a narrowboat.' Nonsense!

One of my biggest concerns was getting through all those locks single-handed; if the carpal tunnel nightmare decided to play up, it could easily be no-handed. I also have quite a debilitating neck injury which comes and goes, not to mention general bits of arthritis here and there. Apart from the potential physical problems, I had no idea how to negotiate a lock on my own. My new next-door neighbour, another Martin, agreed to come out on the cut with me and guide me through the procedure which was very kind of him and an hour or so later with two locks safely cracked, we returned. Just as well because Martin probably had some serious power drinking arranged for the rest of the day. 'Nothing to it really, just take it easy and concentrate'. he assured me. And the best piece of advice – 'never take your eye of the boat.' I felt inclined to go out every day and have a little practice but I realised how pointless that would be. I might as well just set off and I would get all the practice I needed.

The weather right through the spring had been really good. Now it was May and just like in recent years, things looked like they were going backwards. I had intended to set sail in mid-May but now the weather was cool windy and mostly wet with temperatures so low I had the *Morso* stove lit most evenings. In a way, the bad weather was to my advantage because I was full of trepidation at the thought of undertaking something so alien to me.

The last week of May came and the weather was still not quite right but realising that if I was not going to spend the whole summer humming and hawing, I had to make a decision, so I chose the next Tuesday 2nd June, as the day that I would set off. (Looking back, I cannot remember why I choose Tuesday, surely a Monday would have been more appropriate.)

I spent my last day in Watford sorting the various bits and pieces out. Water, fuel and other essentials. I bought a couple of mooring pins and Frank even gave me a few old battered ones just in case. Some weeks later, I found another half a dozen stowed away in a secret locker, along with a magnet on a length of string. The magnet was so powerful it could rip manhole covers out of the road. There were also a few more hammers in there too, you can never have enough.

I spent most of my last evening with my good 'copper' neighbours in the local *Harvester* plastic pub, along with its plastic food and sanitised beer. And that was that – all those years in exile were about to come to an end. Would this be my final attempt to escape from the south of England... permanently? Just before I went to sleep I got that peculiar nostalgic feeling that I always came when I was facing my last night after a few years at an address. Even when I hadn't particularly enjoyed living somewhere, I found that I would become attached and a bit sentimental, though strangely, it never applied when facing a final night's rest in Aldershot. Years ago, when I was about to move from my house in Swindon, there was a drama on TV about a family moving home; I recall the father looking back at their house in the dark, seeing the lights flickering and saying to the family, 'Just think kids there will be no light shining at number thirty-four tomorrow night.' I remember watching it and feeling incredibly sad: I had the same feeling now but then I remembered that this time it did not really apply, because wherever I ended up tomorrow, I would still be in my own bed in my own house as it were. The thought cheered me up and I fell into a drunken sleep.

Chapter 1.

Hemel Hempstead

I had set the alarm to go off at eight and it did. The ducks weren't quacking and tapping on the side of the boat like they normally did. If they had any sense they would be hiding somewhere sheltered; the weather was horrendous the boat was bobbing around like a cork with rain squalling horizontally in the unseasonable gale. I was quite pleased my hangover felt relatively mild and I decided to go and speak to Frank once I had eaten my porridge, done my ablutions and got dressed

Really, I was hoping he would say, 'Oh no mate you can't set off in this weather,' but instead he just looked out of the window and said, 'Hmm, it'll be alright – only a bit of wind – like I said, just take your time, try not to rush things and you'll be fine.' 'Oh yeah, all right.' I replied. So, I shook Frank's hand and thanked him for taking a wad of money off me each month and for letting me stay on his marina. I always think it is best not to burn any bridges when one of life's episodes comes to an end but I do not always succeed.

I went slowly back to *Salamander* and started the vintage Lister engine, which was in fact just one evolution on from Watts's prototype steam engine. Once the clouds of black clag dispersed, it settled down into its usual loud chug. Leaving the engine to warm up properly for a few minutes,

I went inside and donned my thermals and best waterproof fishing gear. My neighbours Stan and Paul had promised the night before that they would come and wave me good bye but it looked like they couldn't be arsed now. So, I sent them a text message to say that I had really gone and began to untie the mooring ropes.

Suddenly I was looking forward to this: I very carefully reversed *Salamander* out of the tight mooring space in a series of to-ing and fro-ing moves, a bit like doing an eight-point turn in a car on a narrow country road. Eventually I was facing the right direction and began slowly chugging forward towards the tee junction exit from the marina and out into on the Grand Union Canal and the wider world. Frank suddenly appeared on his scooter on the little peninsula that jutted out slightly, affording a better view of the blind turn ahead of me and kindly guided me out into the canal. He wished me all the best again and off I went on my journey proper.

I had no time to settle down at all because the first of the 250 + locks that I would have to negotiate lay immediately in front of me. The centre line mooring rope was already arranged along the roof with the end close to hand, along with the windlass to operate the lock paddles. Because I was going uphill the lock was already set for me with the bottom gates open. This meant that I could cruise straight in. Slowing right down, I slipped the engine into neutral, letting the boat find its own way into the lock as I stepped carefully off and walked up the stone steps leading to the top of the lock.

As I got there, I realised that the boat was travelling a bit faster than I had estimated. Also, I had not noticed that I had positioned the rope forward of the cowl for the gas water heater, so that when I took the strain of the moving boat onto the rope, the chimney was immediately ripped from its mounting. I somehow managed to grab it before it rolled into the water; a good start! Closing the gates behind me and ensuring the paddles were closed, I opened the top paddles, allowing water to flow from the gates and thus fill the lock chamber, raising the boat, and just in case that you did not already know, that is how it all works. Once filled, the top gates were opened and I could chug out of the lock. There is no quick way of doing this, each lock takes a minimum of twenty minutes to negotiate – it's a right pain.

Because the Grand Union is a wide beam canal, all the locks are just over fourteen feet wide and can take two boats at a time which can be an advantage when there are other boats around because the work can be shared. Today though, there was just me, in the pouring rain and wind. I had to walk all the way around the locks opening and closing the huge double gates then going back round again to open and close the ratchets which wind the paddles open and closed.

At least all this work was keeping me warm! I just had enough time to straighten my hair before the next lock loomed large. This time however, the gates were closed which meant that I would have to tie the boat to the bollards in the lock pound, then walk forwards to empty the lock and then repeat the same process all over again. This time too, it would take even longer because I would have to let thousands of gallons of water flow out before I could enter the lock only to have to fill it again.

I made certain that the rope was clear of the now fragile cowl and pointed the boat to the left, sorry port, where the bollards were, hoping to get near to the furthest ones, thus reducing the amount of walking to a minimum. Once again, I put her into neutral and stepped off onto the towpath but straight away I knew I had badly underestimated the speed and *Salamander* was moving too fast. Pulling desperately with all my strength, I was now aquaplaning on the soaking wet grass underfoot. This new experience didn't last long, almost instantly I felt the end of the rope slip through my wet gloves and I was rocketed backwards, landing painfully onto the wet grass and pebbles.

Seconds later the boat gave the gates an almighty whack. This would have been severely frowned upon by other boaters had any been mad enough to be around on a day like this. Sorry Canal and River Trust Registered Charity and Quango, it was an accident and I will try not to ever do it again.

After a little grovel on the floor, like one does in these situations, I quickly grabbed the rope again, before *Salamander* could wonder off into the middle of the canal. I got up and had a look around hoping that no one had witnessed this free entertainment, but thankfully there was only me. Then I remembered that the idea was to carefully loop the rope around the steel bollard, avoiding any stray fingers and use that as a fulcrum to slow the boat. I would remember that next time, it was a painfully steep learning curve!

The next lock was situated on the edge of the rather lovely and huge Cassiobury Park which extends almost all the way into Watford town centre a couple of miles away. This particular lock was situated right under a footbridge and normally in decent weather and especially at weekends, the area would be packed with the bridges full of 'gonezoillers' (the aquatic version of train-spotters), all hanging around, waiting for some idiot on a boat to make a spectacular cock-up.

This could well have been me but today because of the weather, there was only a solitary 'chav' on his drug-dealer bike, waiting. I have a bit of a problem with these types – my emotions when I have to deal with them are usually a strange mixture – somewhere between feeling threatened or wanting to deliver a well-aimed throat punch. 'Wanna a hand mate?' it said in west London wannabee gangster talk. I couldn't see his face properly because of his hood but I could still detect the shifty body language. 'Wanna a hand mate?' he repeated. 'No thanks, I'm all right' I said. 'No, it all right, I help yer innit,' he insisted. I wondered why these people always prance around excitedly on the balls of their feet; 'Come on I help, innit' he repeated. In the end I said, 'Alright, push the gate shut for me.' Then he said, 'how far yer go, innit?' I thought he would probably not know where Wales was so I didn't bother to give an answer. All this time I was keeping a sharp eye out for where the windlass was, just in case. Suddenly he remembered he had somewhere more important to go, and said, 'Anyway I gotta go now, innit bro.' as if it had been me who had stopped him and insisted he helped me. He then sped off up the tree-lined path on his stolen BMX bike.

I continued on my way, feeling relieved partly because the 'chav' had gone and also because I had managed to get through this lock unscathed at last. I was now a relatively expert boater.

Soon the canal began to twist and meander, punctuated every few hundred yards by an ornate bridge or yet another lock. All the time I was going past familiar places. I had ridden along this stretch of canal hundreds of times over the years; often the day after a race, I would go for a gentle potter on my mountain bike; this was the acknowledged way to allow the legs to recover. Before anyone tuts and stops reading in disgust, I was always a careful and considerate rider whether on the road or towpath, I have never once jumped a red light or startled a walker or even a duck. The towpath was always littered with fishermen and women and even though I dabble myself when I get the urge, I cannot help noticing most anglers seem to be 'perma-grumpy', whether one is courteous or not and this is not just in the south, it seems to be a nationwide thing. One thing that had intrigued me initially on these rides was seeing signs informing me that it was 74 or 69 miles or whatever to Braunston, depending on how far along I was. At first, I had no idea where Braunston was; evidently *Microsoft Word* spell check does not know either, insisting on drawing a red line under the name of any place name outside of the USA. My geography was generally quite good but I was stumped; perhaps it was the place where the famous brown pickle that every supermarket in the land insists on smearing all over the cheese sandwiches they sell for the extortionate price of £2.80 apiece. Perhaps it started out as Braunston Pickle and over the years we corrupted it to Branston, after all we were quite good at that sort of thing. I decided originally that because of the distances indicated, it was probably somewhere on the outskirts of Birmingham. I know now I was wrong, it was just a fleeting thought, possibly caused by rushing blood. Later I would look on a map and confirm exactly where this little 'City' was.

I had mentioned occasionally to friends that I would like to ride there and back in one day albeit a long one, just for the fun of it. This was something that I would have been quite capable of doing twelve or fifteen years ago. They would usually give me blank looks and I never knew if it was because of the distance involved or because they had no idea where Braunston was either.

I was now passing the grounds of the Grove Hotel, Hertfordshire's premier venue for dining and other leisure activities such as golf. This is the hotel the England football team use before their frequent defeats at Wembley and a few years ago, some of the world's leading psychopaths, such as Obama, Junkers and Cameron came here for the Bilderberg Summit, to discuss and plan where and when the next wars would take place.

I had once enquired about a job at the Grove, though I knew it was way above my capabilities now. I only did it because of someone else's insistence. The executive Head Chef at the time (he may still be), was an infamous ex-army chef called Harry Lomas, who had started out an apprentice tradesman at sixteen and left the army as a major about forty years later. I emailed Harry about working there. I did not know him personally so I kept the email fairly formal, calling Harry sir, etc. but mentioning my own distinguished military career. He replied around an hour later with the greeting, 'Hello mate, yes I am always looking for talented chefs here. I have got ninety at the moment.' Ninety! Harry was very nice about my enquiry, though I got the impression he was tactfully telling me that I was a bit too old to be starting there. Fair enough – ninety chefs though – I wonder if they say grill or salamander?

Looking at the *Collins -Nicholson Waterways Guide,* they make no mention of the Grove. They would probably not want scruffy boat people in there throwing their money around anyway.

By mid-afternoon the rain stopped and the wind died down to just the occasional force eight gusts and then, believe it or not, the sun came out from behind a threatening looking cloud. I had only passed two other boats so far, both of them of the working variety, selling coal and diesel (and possibly marijuana if you asked politely). I was feeling quite pleased with myself by now, I had started to get into a routine in the locks and I had slipped by these other vessels without incident. Not too remarkable really, this was probably the widest stretch of canal in the country.

I had reached the outskirts of Hemel Hempstead when I encountered a lock with gates that refused to open and it didn't help that I was now starting to feel fairly weary. Patience is always needed when negotiating any lock. If the water on both sides of the gate is not perfectly even, it is impossible to move them. Sometimes when the flow through the paddles slows to the last remaining dregs, it is difficult to judge what the balance is. I thought this might be the case here so I waited a few minutes and shoved again but they still wouldn't budge. I waited even longer but still nothing happened. if I keep heaving and straining like this, I thought, someone will come along and find me dead in the water, another unnecessary stroke victim.

There again it might be days before my body was discovered, there wasn't a soul anywhere. Usually on any towing path on any canal in the land, every few minutes a dog walker will appear from thin air. This usually happens when trying to have a discrete 'Jimmy Riddle' in the hedgerow, but today though, nothing. I sat on top of the wooden gate in the now blazing sun and thought about how embarrassing it would be if I reappeared travelling in reverse gear back in Watford just as the sun was setting.

I decided to give Paul the 'copper' a call, he would be at work now and probably chasing armed robbers around the M25 but I thought it was justified though – they were there to help after all. I was a bit surprised at first when Paul's 'oppo' Andy answered the call; 'All right mate yeah? Paul's driving at the moment, I'll get him to call you back when we get to McDonalds, we've got a lot on at the moment you know.' I thanked him and sat there wondering a bit more about the possible reasons why the lock wouldn't cooperate.

Eventually Paul called me back; 'Have you checked that all the paddles are closed?' I told him they were. 'Has the lock chamber stopped filling yet?' 'Yes, it has.' 'Have you tried rocking the gate gently?' I said I had done that too. 'What about emptying the lock and refilling it?' I said I had already tried that but the gates were still solid. I was half expecting him to ask me to confirm that the plug was in the socket and that the power was switched on.

'If I were you I would try emptying it and refilling it again mucker but if that doesn't work, I don't know what to suggest.' Suddenly he remembered; 'Oh yeah, we had trouble with that one, it's a swine. What you need to do is give it a bit of a nudge with the front of your boat. Paul then added; 'Try that and give me a shout later to let me know how you get on. If the worst comes to the worst I finish my shift at ten.'

This was reassuring; it meant he would get home about eleven and another hour could see him with me (or if he came out on his boat it would be about three the next morning). With no need to panic, I followed my friend's advice – and with the gentlest of pushes, both gates swung fully open as if to say, 'We have no idea what the problem was.' Finally, I was free to continue the last couple of miles to the first overnight stop of my long journey.

Soon I was going under an eerie looking railway bridge which was so skewed that it ran almost parallel to the canal. Just as I was about to disappear into the cavern, a Virgin Express train screamed overhead at some outrageous speed. I remember thinking that it would probably be in Birmingham or Manchester before I got to Hemel Hempstead, just up the road. I had a little daydream about what the scene would have looked like in the days of steam trains.

A sign informed me that this was Nash Mills where, just like lots of towns in this area, papermaking had been a major industry years ago. There were lots of lovely birch trees in the Chilterns to feed the mills. I had started the day counting the locks as each one was conquered but I had long since forgotten what the tally was. I can confirm now though, after looking at my map that there were still five more to go.I was in Hemel Hempstead proper now, a town I knew quite well but from the perspective of the canal everything looked so different. Chugging slowly past the new-ish council owned marina, I recalled one afternoon a year ago, when I had walked with Stan all the way from Watford to this very point in blazing afternoon sun – around seven miles each way. We then turned around and walked straight back, just for fun. It was getting dark when we eventually got back and we collapsed in the Harvester plastic pub for some well-earned but dubious looking food. I bet the Harvester chefs don't know about Salamanders.

There were just two more locks to go today and these came in quick succession which was just as well, as I had begun to feel slightly lock punch drunk. I spotted a likely looking gap between a line of boats although the towpath was far from busy. I could have parked anywhere but I noticed that Tesco wasn't very far away and there were a few things I required, some cans of beer being at the top of the list. Don't be getting the wrong idea, I drank very little during this entire voyage but tonight I thought I deserved a reward and besides, I was spitting feathers. Once Salamander was safely moored, I got the kettle on, made a brew and got down to one of most the most satisfying things that I know . Whenever I have gone on any kind of adventure I always get a good feeling pouring over a map and recalling all the places visited that day. I still remember the frustration of being dumped once in some god-forsaken hole in Norway in the snow with no idea where we were. I wasn't in a position of power at the time and I couldn't get hold of a map to satisfy my curiosity for several days.

It was also interesting to look at where I had arrived relative to neighbouring places. This ritual always felt particularly good if I had arrived under my own steam, be it bike or on foot. I had a great feeling of job satisfaction now. Granted there was an engine involved but there had been a lot of human effort expended too. Due to the amount of time I had been on the move, I felt as if I should be in another country by now. The distance I had covered in six hours was actually only around eight miles but that sounds more respectable when you realise that included in that meagre distance were twenty-one locks and I had operated every damned one of them myself (my 'chav' friend didn't actually do anything except talk a lot and spring up and down on his toes). I was absolutely knackered but what a satisfying day.

After a shower, I got dressed in some normal looking clothes and set off for Tesco, which was only about 400 yards away which just as well because my legs felt like lead, and my neck and shoulders were also hurting badly after a day of over use. Once I had completed my bit of shopping I thought that I would give Simon a call to let him know how the day had panned out. I sat outside on a bench relaying all the little incidents that had occurred during the six-hour voyage. When I finished talking I put the phone away and looked around to see a woman staring at me with a look of disgust on her face. No, I was not in another country, I was most definitely still in southeast England and would be for a few days yet.

I can't really remember much about the rest of that evening apart from thinking how strange it was, seeing a constant stream of dog walkers going past the boat which never happened in the marina. I had a bit of a fret, wondering if I would be left in peace and quiet and the last thing I remember was trying to get into a comfortable position in bed so that my neck and shoulders didn't hurt too much – and then it was Wednesday morning!

Chapter 2

Berkhamstead

Generally speaking, I have never been one for lying in my 'pit' all day. I am usually up around seven or eight most mornings but over the last few years, once I am up, I have got into the habit just sitting around for ages drinking endless cups of tea before actually doing anything. On this second fine day, I had the thought that really, I don't have to do anything to be doing, what it is that I am supposed to be doing! I could start the engine make a cup of tea take it up to the stern and be on my way almost instantly, while I slowly fully woke up and came around. Of course, this would only work if there were no locks immediately ahead and there were lots of them waiting for me today. Still I made a little agreement with myself that I would try and do this in future rather than wasting half of my day.

I was pleasantly surprised when the *Lister* engine fired immediately, coming to life as readily as my car's engine. Normally it would whine and splutter for around twenty seconds, then begin a very slow chug, before threatening to die, until it was given a life-saving burst of red diesel which would produce a huge, embarrassing cloud of black smoke. After this it would settle down and chug forever more, so much so that I could even turn the ignition off and the engine would just keep going.

I put my *Collins-Nicholson Waterways Guide* on top of the hatch above the engine compartment (this probably had some nautical name but I neither knew or cared what it was), so that all I had to do was glance down to be able to see where I was on the map. Also to hand were the essential windlass, gloves, not for the cold but to protect my delicate hands, the unfurled centre rope and of course, the vital mug of tea.

Away I cruised towards the first lock of the day en-route to Berkhamstead. I knew that there was an electrically operated swing bridge that had to be crossed not too far away and I was already a bit anxious regarding this structure; I wasn't quite sure what to expect, except that I knew it involved quite a lot of button pushing. It was a lovely sunny day and the sky looked especially blue after yesterday's 'monsoon'. Everything was sparkling, the ducks were quacking again and I felt unusually cheerful. The three locks I had already passed through had presented no dramas and my map showed that I would be soon approaching Winkwell swing bridge. A few minutes later I could actually see the bridge across the water, just as I had expected; this was the bridge's default position because of the high volume of traffic crossing over it.

Suddenly I remembered the security key which I would need to operate the mechanism. These keys were issued to boat licence holders and because Sheila had let me continue the use of her licence until it expired, I had not even thought about it until now. I knew there were loads of bits and pieces on the end of cork balls dangling on various hooks in the engine compartment amongst the hammers and coal shovels and I was sure that I had seen a likely looking key on one of these.

Slowing down, I decided I would stop and moor briefly so that I could find it but at that moment, a boat half the size of mine appeared from nowhere and instantly overtook me. The driver smiled at me and asked if I was all right; then he said, 'Stay on your boat mate, I'll do the bridge for you.' and with that, he shot off at a speed I suspected was well above the regulation four miles per hour. True to his word, the bridge was swung well clear by the time I chugged past it; my new friend waved me on saying, 'Stay there mate I'll sort it.'

All this benevolence gave me a lovely warm feeling; especially when I looked to my left as I passed and saw the long line of BMWs, Mercedes and Audi cars complete with impatient drivers waiting to get to the 'Des Res' homes off the track after the bridge. Better still, I was also pleased to see that another boat was approaching from the other direction so they would have to wait even longer.

I cannot remember an awful lot about the remainder of the morning; there were another five or so locks to get through and then I was in to the outskirts of Berkhamstead or 'Berko' as some of the locals refer to it. This medium-sized commuter town has one or two claims to fame. In 1066 after a bit of a disagreement at the seaside in Hastings, the Saxons signed the surrender to William the Conqueror right here in 'Berko' castle' (I'm sure that Mr Junker would have approved!) What else? In the 19th century, it was the hub for the entire national canal system and further towards the town, I passed under a bridge adorned with a fancy sign proclaiming 'Port of Berkhamstead'.

The most impressive thing about 'Berko' though, was the fact that it was home to Frank – Frank from the marina – remember? Allegedly, he could get from Watford to here on his boat in some mind-bogglingly quick nine hours. He had a posse of heavies that would go ahead and sort out all the locks for him and it was by all accounts, a very well-choreographed routine. Maybe he had a few mates in the local fire stations too, who moonlighted with a borrowed fire engine to help fill the locks quicker.

This was another place I had visited several times but now I didn't recognise any of it. The canal threaded its way right through the middle of the town, sneaking behind old higgledy-piggledy backs in a blend of houses, pubs, bridges and of course locks: on my right were the ruins of the castle next door to the railway station and it all looked wonderful. It must be great to earn around £120K a year and be able to live there. I had only travelled this route on a train twice, each time on my way from Euston to Blackpool to the world's biggest magic convention and I tried to recall why I had not noticed the castle and the canal scene from the train. I then remembered the first time was because I was on a course of Fluoxetine to prevent me from slashing my boss's jugular vein and by the time we screamed through Berkhamstead, I was fast asleep dribbling on the shoulder of the poor unknown woman sitting next to me. The second time, I was conscious however the train was going so fast that everything outside was just a blur.

At one lock, thoughtfully placed right next to a pub garden, I had to mark time because another boat was already in the lock travelling in the opposite direction. I did a bit of heaving and cranking to help and had a brief conversation with the three young lads and the girl on board. They said they had already been to John O'Groats or some distant destination and now they were on the way back to Camden. The most sociable of them, began recommending a pub to me but I interrupted, saying I didn't intend staying here tonight, that I was hoping to get closer to Tring. He went on to say this pub didn't look like a pub until you got inside and even then, you couldn't be sure it actually was a pub. He then made some reference to 'Schrodinger's cat' and looked quite pleased when I replied that I found Quantum Physics interesting too. So, we said our goodbyes and I reassured him that he would probably be able to get a re-supply of magic mushrooms in Camden. The sun continued to shine.

Just as I was about to disembark to travel the 500 yards to the next lock, a foreign sounding man approached me, he asked if I was going through the lock. Resisting the temptation for a sarcastic response and say unless he knew of a different route then yes, I would be. He then explained that his young son had never seen anything like this in his life; and would I be kind enough to explain and demonstrate to the boy how a lock worked. If they had asked me a few weeks earlier they would have been disappointed but now I answered that not only would I oblige their request but if they liked, I would give them a ride to it. I strategically placed the two of them either side of me and off we chugged. The boy was about nine I guessed, his face was a picture and I liked to think I had probably made the youngster's day.

We chatted on the way to the lock and I discovered they were a German family from somewhere in Bavaria who were in the UK for a couple of weeks holiday. The dad spoke excellent English, like most Europeans do these days; This saved me from having to embarrass myself by trying to recite the one and only German tongue twister that I knew:

Esel essen nesseln
Aber nesseln essen esel nicht

Donkeys eat nettles
But nettles don't eat donkeys

This doesn't work nearly as well translated into English! It was quite difficult trying to speak above the noise that the Lister engine was making and the father asked me if it had originally come from a tractor which made me smile a bit. I said no it was a dedicated marine engine but I knew what he meant. When I was a little boy, my mates and I would occasionally witness a strange procession of ancient farm machinery being transported back from the fields to the farm where it all lived. A strange-looking tractor always pulled this bizarre show. More like a steam traction engine than diesel tractor, with a huge whirling flywheel. The noise it made was absolutely deafening and was guaranteed to stop us from bird nesting, or setting fire to another field of dried grass for a few minutes. It sounded very similar to my boat. I later discovered it was a Field Marshall tractor, they were built in Gainsborough in Lincolnshire. To start the engine each day a detonator and a burning fuse would be inserted down into the exhaust pipe to fire the beast into its cacophony!

I had begun looking for a likely spot to tie up the boat as we approached the lock, the bottom gates of which were closed when suddenly a tall man dressed in dungarees and a '*Crocodile Dundee*' hat appeared from nowhere. I thought that he was going to join the three of us already on the deck but he stopped just short of it. He was so close that I could smell the Foie Gras that he had eaten for lunch and I thought he was perhaps about to attack me. Instead he just said, 'You can't go any further.' Rather than Australian, I detected upper middle-class Home Counties; staring at him I said, 'Why can't I go any further? ('You odious man' – I didn't say the last part, just thought it.) He repeated himself, 'You can't go any further.' 'Yeah, I heard you the first time', I said; 'what's the problem?'

Calming slightly and a little more civilly, he answered, 'The lock ahead is broken and there is a queue – you are sixth in it so you will just have to wait.' In my best sarcastic tone, I replied; 'I'm sorry mate but my crystal ball is away getting repaired at the moment, how could I know that the lock wasn't working?' The two bewildered Germans had now jumped off the boat and re-joined the rest of the family who had walked alongside us as it would have been pushing things to accommodate them all on the stern deck, trying to get them to duck and weave in unison to avoid the ever-swinging tiller whilst I steered.

'Dundee' as if completely deaf, just repeated; 'There's a queue and you will have to wait.' I had meant to have a little parting conversation with the Germans but because of Dundee's aggressive interruption, they gave me a bit of an embarrassed wave and scarpered. This had all taken a few seconds and I was a bit confused about what to do now. I obviously couldn't go forwards anywhere and glancing behind, as well as the six boats my new friend had mentioned, there were quite a lot of other boats scattered here and there.

The location was generally quite compact and confined in a narrow cutting with a low bridge just to the rear, there wasn't anywhere for me to go. So, I just let the overflow from the lock in front push me backwards so that I came to rest with my stern hard against the very expensive looking bow of his boat which had some reference to Aylesbury written on its side. His wife was sitting in the cratch area reading *Horse and Hound* magazine I gave her an apology for touching their property; she snarled that it was alright, but I could see it was anything but.

After ensuring that *Salamander* was safely tied to the bank, I stepped on to the towpath to see for myself what the problem was and sure enough, the lock was buggered. The huge post supporting the gate had popped out of its submerged hole like a massive dislocated shoulder. The Canal and River people had already dispatched a vanload of men to try and repair it and they were busy scratching their heads when I got to them.

Apart from the workmen, most of the occupants from the other stranded boats were looking at the scene with everyone giving their opinions to each other. I said something helpful and was totally ignored. By now I had sussed that my 'friend' was in the company of another, equally obnoxious couple. These two were quieter than the others.

In fact, they didn't speak one word to me throughout. I noticed that they also owned a million-pound narrowboat.

There was nothing anyone could do to help the workmen, besides I suspected that most of the observers didn't do manual labour, so we all eventually slunk off back to our respective boats and waited – and waited. I foolishly attempted to make conversation with my next-door neighbours. She was still reading the magazine and he now had the *Daily Telegraph* folded on his knee, going through the crossword so fast that the pen was starting to smoke. I cannot remember what I said, but they completely ignored me so I stopped bothering and went inside, deciding to cook myself a particularly smelly curry. So that they could appreciate it, I opened all the doors and windows, I didn't want them thinking that I lived on pot noodles and crisps. After three hours, the lock was repaired so we all got ready to depart and like a mug, I volunteered to help all the other boats get through I was last in the queue anyway. Because of my generosity, 'Dundee' now felt obliged to have a bit of a conversation with me and asked me how far I was going and I told him, North Wales. I had expected that maybe a few of the crew members from the flotilla to hang back and help me sort out the lock, once they were all through it. Did they? No, they just got onto their boats and pissed off into the distance. It was now around six o'clock and I realised that there was no way that I could get to Tring today.

I say Tring, although the canal just like its railway, doesn't actually go there and more accurately, Tring summit was where I was hoping to get to. Consulting my canal guidebook once more, I could see that there were three more locks over a distance of about one mile and once through these, I would be at Northchurch. I was feeling pretty tired again by now and decided this village would be my final destination for today. I tied *Salamander* to the mooring pins that I had just hammered into the grassy border along the towpath. placing half a tennis ball on top of each pin, ensuring that any careless joggers didn't accidentally leave a kneecap or shin bone behind on the sharp battered top edges.

I suddenly recognised the road bridge a few hundred yards ahead, realising I had ridden over it dozens of times in the past. The road formed part of the route of many of my longer training rides. It led to the Ashridge Estate on the edge of the Dunstable Downs, overlooking the attractive village of Aldbury...where just like Berkhamstead, it costs a fortune to live.

After a shower and a meal, I got the generator going again – unlike most boats *Salamander* had no inverters on board. These are clever gadgets which turn twelve volts of direct current into 240 volts alternating current and I had mentioned them to Sheila but of course, she had no idea what I was talking about.

The main reason I needed mains power was so I could get my PC going and post informative comments and pictures onto *Facebook* each day. It was only day two but I was already pleasantly surprised by the number of encouraging comments I had received yesterday. Some of the comments came from people I hadn't heard from in ages and a few were from people I had never heard of! Over the coming days and weeks, along with a log, this became a daily ritual and I looked forward to writing and posting it each evening. The captain's log became the basis of what you are reading now (for those of you who are still conscious!).

Around 10 pm. it was just getting dark and was now a fine pleasant evening. Looking up from the computer monitor, I could hardly believe what I saw: the doors at the rear of the boat were ajar and through the gap was the biggest full moon that I have ever seen. It was gorgeous as it slowly rose above the horizon, creating a mirror image reflection in the perfectly still canal. I wanted to go running along the towpath knocking on the windows of all the other boats there, telling people to look outside but I wisely decided this was probably not a good idea. I spent the rest of the evening looking outside every half hour or so to see how the moon was progressing and checking no-one had stolen it.

Chapter 3

Pitstone

Just after eight the next morning, I slipped my mooring as the nautically afflicted people say and I was away, with a mug of tea in hand. I was just starting to go under the road bridge, that I mentioned earlier when I came to an unexpected lock virtually underneath it. It wasn't as if someone had put it there last night just for a laugh, it had obviously been there for a hundred plus years. It was unexpected because when I had looked at my *Collins -Nicholson Waterways Guide*, there was no mention of it. I had not noticed that the relevant bit of the map was straddled across where the pages joined. There was a white strip about a quarter of a mile wide obliterating all the detail running north to south through most of Hertfordshire. I had not noticed this anomaly until now and realised if there was some really vital information omitted (like a lock). it was just tough, making the canal guide somewhat pointless. When I got to the lock it was full so I had to empty it, shunt the boat in, close the gates and fill it all over again. I didn't mind too much though; the sun was shining and the setting in general was delightful.

Apart from all this eye candy, a very pleasant and rather attractive woman walking her dog stopped to chat to me; asking lots of questions about my journey and about canals and boats in general. I thought it was a bit odd that if she walked her dog along the same route every morning, yet she seemed to know so little about canals – perhaps no one had ever spoken to her before!

There was only one more lock to go through before arriving at the curiously named Cowroast (I suppose this relieved the monotony of having a hog roast every Saturday evening if the weather was good). This place was steeped in history; It had once been a Roman settlement and lots of interesting artefacts were found here when the marina was excavated. The place had been on the drover's route and one of the more disturbing finds was a load of cow bones. The name Cowroast apparently was a corruption of Cow Rest.

There was not much here; a pub called, not surprisingly, The Cowroast, a few cottages plus a garage and filling station. Apart from these, there was just the marina, with a well-equipped shop selling rope, lifejackets, outboard engines, anchors, hooks and wooden legs etc. Pretty much all the things that Sheila had kindly left me on *Salamander*. The only thing they didn't sell was food. I was hungry, so I set off for the garage and found myself next to the A4251, the busiest stretch of road I had ever seen. It is amazing how just a few days away from the madding crowd can change one's perceptions. It was as if a busy road, thirty miles from London was the last thing I expected. 'Oh look – cars!' I had to walk along this road to get to the garage, keeping a sharp lookout for speeding vehicles. There wasn't any footpath and drivers wouldn't be expecting to have to swerve around some idiot dressed as a tree (I was still wearing my camouflaged fishing jacket, even though it hadn't rained for a couple of days now). I had to step on and off the road constantly in between convoys of traffic but after about thirty minutes, I returned with my Cheese Ploughman's sandwich – which naturally contained 'Braunston Pickle'.

Halfway back, I came across three young men dressed in suits who looked even more out of place than I did. They seemed respectable and pleasant enough and one of them asked me if I knew where Amersham was. They said they had come from Stoke on Trent to collect a car from an address there and had got off the train at Tring, a good mile away. Their faces dropped when I told them they had a considerable walk to their destination and I didn't have the heart to tell them there was also a perfectly good railway station in Amersham.

I decided to replenish *Salamander's* water tank while I was here but first I would have to buy a key. I mentioned these universal keys earlier; they allow access to all the facilities along any canal; swing bridges, toilets, waste disposal and chastity belts etc. I had thought there was one on the boat but had not been able to find it. I asked the girl in the chandlery shop if they sold such things. She smiled at me and confirmed that they did and that I could buy one for the very reasonable price of six quid. I was thinking to myself that after the earlier conversation with the dog walker, maybe I had been going to all the wrong places for the last seventeen years. If I had looked more carefully, I might have discovered that the women of Hertfordshire were in fact, the friendliest you could find anywhere. Living in the marina, there were always a couple of communal hosepipes around for us to fill our tanks, so I had not had to worry about the mechanics and this was another thing I had overlooked and didn't have a clue about. Back on the towing path, to use the correct term, I laid out my inherited array of hose pipe bits and pieces on the ground; there were about eight of these connectors, all looking very similar with just slight differences. It would have made a good task for the contestants on the 90's TV mind boggle show *The Krypton Factor.*

I asked a man who was walking along by the boat, if he knew which nozzle I needed to connect the hose to the tap. He grunted and said, 'Oh I don't know, I'm not a boater, I am just taking my dog for a walk.' I apologised for not knowing what the rules were, perhaps only people dressed as trees on boats were allowed to make enquiries of others in the same predicament. He must have felt a bit guilty though, because after walking a few paces he turned back and deigned to show me which part I needed to fit to get my water. 'Thank you, Sir,'.

I was feeling quite excited today; according to the canal guide book, I would triumph over Tring Summit and I had visions of glorious views of the Vale of Aylesbury and perhaps beyond to the Cotswolds.

I was now going up a dead straight cutting, lined by huge trees coming right down to the water and even standing in it in places. It was quite eerie, there was no one around and the engine sounded louder than normal, echoing off the cutting sides. I thought a brew might help relieve the monotony and because there wasn't anyone to be seen guessed I could duck inside and put the kettle on without bothering to tie the boat up (after all, this was a canal and not some white-water rapids). Slowing down to a crawl, the boat drifted gently towards the bank and when I was sure it was quite stationary, I shot down below, poured about half a pint of water into the kettle and lit the gas.

This procedure took perhaps thirty seconds at the most but dashing back up on deck, I was shocked to find that *Salamander* had managed to arrange herself at a forty-five-degree angle right across the canal and I only just got her straightened out when a boat appeared around the bend at the end of the cutting. I had to moor up properly later, so that I could rescue the by now, dried up and glowing kettle.

A few more hundred yards and I was at the much-anticipated Tring Summit Level but after three days and forty-one ascending locks, at an altitude of 395 above sea level, I was disappointed to find no vistas of distant vales and hills, there were just a few featureless, flat fields. The day got more interesting after lunch though, when I arrived at Bulbourne Junction. There were very few people about but the place still felt exciting with locks, dry docks, footbridges and boats everywhere. There were several reservoirs next to the canal which are used to feed water constantly into the Grand Union, ensuring that it didn't run dry. Apparently, each time a boat passes the summit it will have drawn off something like 200,000 gallons of water! The old canal workshops, complete with a clock tower, gave the place an important feeling and the whole scene reminded me of an old railway locomotive depot. It also marked the start of another series of locks...oh good!

I felt a bit anxious as I slowly approached. I did not know if I should turn left or go around to the right, I noticed a signpost saying that Braunston was 55 miles to the north.

If I had come all the way from the southern end of the canal, I would now be 33 1/2 miles from Brentford and I realised the route I needed curved off to the right. This was quite a complicated arrangement because there was a footbridge straddling the beginning of the Wendover branch, the bridge ran parallel and next to the lock that I was about to go through. I tied *Salamander* to the bollards before the first lock and stood for a few moments thinking that something was different until suddenly the penny dropped. Of course, I was going downhill now. I had got quite comfortable with the uphill locking routine and now I had to start all over learning a new one and my confidence plummeted. The weather had turned warm, even hot now and I did not relish the thought of working seven locks with only just enough time between them for me to catch my breath. A young chap with a toddler was standing on the bridge and we had a bit of a conversation. I told him what I was doing and he must have felt sorry for me and helped a while with the lock.

I knew this area really well from my cycling days but again, it looked completely alien from this canal perspective. Some of the names of the surrounding villages were alien sounding too, Startops, Marsworth and Astral Clinton; I wondered if they have space cadet conventions here? Actually the last one is really called Aston Clinton which is still a wonderful name.

I was just negotiating the fourth lock which was around a bend, when I was startled to see a boat, no two boats appearing behind me in the previous lock. I wondered where the hell they had come from; there weren't any boats near me when I had left Bulborne! I saw a familiar looking figure striding towards me in dungarees and an Aussie hat with his windlass held in the crook of his elbow enabling him to eat his ice cream with ease, as if to say, 'It's a boiling hot day and I have got an ice cream but you have not, peasant – therefore I am superior to you.'

People who whisk their tea and coffee frantically when a simple stir will suffice have always been a source of irritation for me as well as those who attempt to remove the pattern from the plate, making rapid scraping movements with a knife after eating a meal in order to show their appreciation or greed. What's that about? That's what this person was doing now, with his little wooden ice cream paddle. (years ago, I attended a six-session course of counselling (to help me to suffer fools) but it didn't achieve much). The last time I had seen this shower, they were vanishing off into the sun after they left me to fend for myself at the broken lock at Berkhamstead. But that was the day before, so how could they be behind me now? They wouldn't be behind for much longer; for a moment I thought that they would actually leapfrog my boat with theirs – how could they be moving through these locks so quickly? They were defying physics and making their water flow faster than mine. I was starting to feel a bit overwhelmed; I had never been bullied by a narrow boat before. I was just about to get off my vessel to operate the gates again, when 'Dundee' said, 'stay on your boat, we'll do it.'

I asked how it was possible for them to do these canal shape-shifting manoeuvres and at first, he tried to dismiss me, saying; 'Whhaat,' like posh people sometimes do to verbally push people aside. I repeated my question; 'Oh, we went to Wendover,' he said, turning his back to me. So, they had gone all the way up the arm, turned around and sneaked (or is it snuck) up behind me, somehow covering twelve miles more than me. Not that it mattered but I was curious – that would be a full day's cruising for me. I did not have to get off *Salamander* as my intergalactic traveller friends worked the remaining locks before me. Just when I was thinking they were probably alright really and I should stop being so judgemental 'Mr Smug Dundee' after successfully scraping the last of the wax coating off his ice cream tub, peered down into the lock at me and asked; 'Are you new to this?' I replied that yes, I was relatively new to it. 'You do know that it is good etiquette to close the top gates after you have left?' This was because I had left the top gates of the first two locks in this flight undone, out of sheer 'couldn't be arsedness'. There is no excuse but I must also add that one or two people (My ex neighbour Martin being one of them) had implied that this was semi-okay when travelling alone. I said, 'Yes I do know, but like I told you yesterday, I have got over 200 miles and over 250 locks to do on my own, and besides its fifty-fifty.' 'Whhaat?' I went on, explaining that if a boat was coming the other way, it would be in its crew's favour; 'Its fifty-fifty mate.' I finished. 'Yes – but – ha – uhm.' he replied but I missed the last bit; they were out of earshot by then and gone. Of course, the only reason they had apparently helped me was because I was in their way.

The canal meandered all over the meadows through these seven locks; I noticed a solitary house on one of the bends and thought how peaceful it would be to live there.

The next junction was more straightforward than the last. This time the diversion to the left went to Aylesbury, just over six miles away. If I hadn't been paying attention to the map, I could have easily been lulled into thinking that the mountaineering was over for the day. The fiendish canal builders had obviously become bored after building the first seven of the Marsworth locks, so they had a rest for about a mile and then built two more. These two locks were totally isolated and I couldn't see anything other than fields, water, locks, a house – and two huge ginger dogs – I went through the by now, familiar drill and the lock was set for me, so I sailed straight in.

I am not that familiar with dogs, so I couldn't say what make they were. They were lean and muscular though, and more troubling, they weren't messing around wasting energy with pointless barking like less serious predators tend to. The two beasts were on my right, so I could operate the left-hand gate safely but that was no use; somehow, I had to get across and close the other gate too. Not knowing how agile the dogs were, I was concerned they might be able to leap clean over the short space and savage me on the roof of my own boat. They were obviously fighting fit, keeping up constant shuttle runs back and forth along the side of the lock. I knew all about shuttle runs; I had spent a considerable amount of time as a soldier doing them in various gymnasiums worldwide. Unlike me though, these two did not collapse in a heap on the floor after five minutes of exertion.

Every now and then they ran off and vanished and this worried me even more. I was convinced they knew a secret route from their side to mine and I hid in the engine compartment with a windlass, ready to try and defend myself from the 'Baskerville' duo if they sneaked up on me. I was getting really annoyed now – someone must own them – it was not as if this was private property – people came along here all the time. A jogger came past and must have known about the dogs because he increased his pace when he was within the killing zone. I said something about them to him but he just mumbled and ran away; I wouldn't have stopped for a chat either.

I had been trapped here now for well over an hour and these monsters were still sprinting up and down the path. I began to study their behaviour more carefully and realised that when they disappeared round the back of the house, it was possibly because they had found something else of interest to distract them, rather than having a meeting to discuss how to sneak up on me and spring an ambush. I waited until they disappeared again and made a run for it. As I went around to their side of the lock, I could feel the adrenalin coursing through me and the hairs on the back of my neck were tingling. I decided if they returned suddenly, my only chance would be to jump into the canal. Hopefully they would be poor swimmers although I doubted it. Needless to say, once I was clear of the lock I did not bother going back to close the gates.

I had almost reached next lock by the time the dogs returned, looking even angrier now as they realised I had outsmarted them. I noticed there was quite a substantial hedge at the bottom of the garden which looked like it might form a barrier, preventing them from getting to the next lock. They were still charging up and down but stopping at the hedge before repeating it all again. They could probably have leapt this hedge if they had been hungry enough but thankfully, they were beginning to lose heart and knew I was about to make a break for freedom. I didn't close the last lock gate either.

I cruised for about another mile to where a few other boats were already moored and decided to call it a day. I judged I would probably be safe here and the hounds wouldn't sneak out after dark to stalk me. I made myself a strong mug of tea to calm my nerves, deciding that I would write a stiff letter to the Canal and River Trust people, complaining that I don't pay the best part of a thousand quid a year in licence fees to be harassed by ginger dogs and telling them to get a grip! I never did though.

Later that day, catching up on my captain's log and map reading ritual, I saw I had chosen to anchor for the night, just outside the village of Pitstone, situated almost at the foot of Ivinghoe Beacon, the prominent landmark that rises to 757 ft. above the sea. Both the Icknield Way and Ridgeway long distance footpaths cross it and I had often dripped profusely with sweat after cycling over the top of it, on many occasions in my past life.

Looking to the north was the village of Cheddington, where in August 1963, Bruce Reynolds, Buster Edwards and sixteen of their mates stopped the overnight Glasgow to London mail train and helped themselves to approximately 2.5 million pounds. I vaguely remember, watching this on black and white TV and people talked about the audacity of the crime for months afterwards. I also remember thinking at the time that I didn't have a clue where Buckinghamshire was.

Studying my canal guide again, just to see if the two angry dogs got a mention. I noticed that the map once again omitted lots of detail surrounding the locks. You can imagine how surprised I was to find that the house that I describe in the incident doesn't exist, look as I did it isn't shown at all. The only thing that is featured, other than the two locks, are a couple of contour lines. I only mention this because I am concerned that if you decided to check, you might be inclined to think that I had invented the dog story. Looking back, I can't remember a single thing about that evening or the night. the fact that I am writing about it confirms that the dogs didn't come looking for me as the clouds flittered across the near full moon!

Chapter 4

Soulbury

It was hard to believe that it was now already Friday. Of course, setting off on Tuesday rather than Monday had helped to trick my mind. I had no TV as such, just a 'dongle' which plugged into the back of my PC and I didn't feel like starting the generator just so I could watch Carol Kirkwood greeting us all with her over enthusiastic 'Good morrrnning' while she regaled us with the weekend weather. . It fascinated and annoyed me in equal measures whenever she mispronounced northern as *northeren* and southern as *southeren*. I supposed this eccentricity might be to remind us she was Scottish and imagined her director hissing into her earpiece – 'You said it again Carol!' Instead I just listened to Radio Two on my hissing, crackling wind-up DBS radio for a few minutes to hear the eight o'clock news headlines then I promptly silenced it before 'Evans' wound me up for the rest of the day.

As I approached the Great Seabrook swing bridge, two other small boats, a plastic cruiser and a miniature narrow boat about twenty feet long, had just gone past., Both skippers saw me coming and beckoned me through and I thanked them both. There was a lock a little further on and as I could see there nothing coming the other way, I went in and waited; both the other vessels were so short, all three of us could fit in and it would have been rude for me to go through alone after they had helped me past the bridge. Besides it was good to have some company. Also, to get my 'green' hat on for a second, it was a good way to earn brownie points – just like sharing a bath, it saved water! Both boats bobbed into the lock beside me and we began the now familiar ball-aching tasks involved. After the first lock, my two new mates did all of the work through the next three or four locks, insisting that I stayed on my boat, so all I had to do was steer. Unlike yesterday's 'company', these two were genuinely pleased to help.

It turned out that they both delivered boats to various destinations for owners unable to do it themselves for whatever reasons. I guessed that one was about my age – late fifties or early sixties – the other was perhaps in his late thirties. The older man looked as rough as a butcher's dog but was surprisingly well spoken while the younger was bigger and looked like a shorthaired hippy though he had a 'Don't mess with me' look.

They asked where I was going and instantly gave the impression they knew exactly where Chirk was when I told them. They then asked which way I intended to go once I got up around the bottom end of Birmingham. 'Good question' I replied; – I had not yet decided. My dilemma was, that once I reached Braunston (oh yes, the legendary Braunston), I then had a choice of going southwest around Britain's second city, or going the longer way, to the east on the North Oxford Canal. Ray, the younger of the two, immediately advised the eastern route; it might be longer but I would spare myself struggling through dozens and dozens of vicious locks and not only that but would also avoid the horrors of Wolverhampton. I wasn't sure if he was talking about structures or the residents. he went on to say the old working boats always took the longer route so I agreed if it was good enough for them, it would be good enough for me.

By now, the elder of the two had left, turning off to an unknown destination leaving just Ray and me. We continued sharing the work between us through another three or four locks and he was excellent company. We were having a great conversation and I told Ray about my unpleasant encounters over the last few days. 'F*** em,' he said; 'Karma mate, they'll get their f***** Karma.' Again, he insisted; 'F*** em, they are the one percent mate – the one percent – try not to let the one percent spoil it for you mate.' In between this advice and my chuckles, Ray would disappear now and then behind a clump of bushes or a hedgerow along the towpath and I assumed he had a weak bladder but after returning for around the sixth time, he said; 'I'm looking for my cat mate – it went missing about three weeks ago the missus is heartbroken.' I liked him even more now and we carried on putting the world to rights. About the only thing we differed on was shutting the top lock gates when boating alone: I mentioned yesterday's 'conversation' about my bad lock drills. 'If I were you mate, I wouldn't worry about it – going all that way on your own – I don't bother half the time.' Just to prove the point, he left the next pair of gates wide open.

Just as we drifted out of the next lock side by side, I committed a cardinal sin. I was having such a good time chatting to my new friend that I lost concentration for a moment – just long enough for the mooring rope I had let go of, to find its way into *Salamander's* propeller. The engine stopped instantly and I knew immediately what had happened: for a second I remember thinking if I ignored the problem it would untangle itself – but of course it wouldn't. Ray had not seen what had happened at first, just that I had stopped halfway out of the lock; when I told him that the rope was in the propeller he just said, 'It's alright mate, no problem. We'll just drift out of the lock then sort it out.' He asked me if I knew what to do and I said yes, I had a vague idea but I had never dismantled a weed hatch myself, though I had heard some right horror stories about sinking boats and the like. I was doing a bit of cursing now but Ray reiterated; 'It's no problem mate – bugger me, a weed hatch is nothing – everything and anything has happened to me since I have been doing this job.' And continued telling me about the number of locks he had fallen into over the years.

A weed hatch – for those of you (Sheila) who could not tell one from a sacrificial anode – - is a metal box that sits just above the waterline over the top of a boat's propeller. There is a bit of variation in design but they are without exception, always located in the most awkward, darkest, claustrophobic, least accessible, most-likely-to-bang-your-head place on a boat.

To the casual passer-by it must have looked like Ray was one of those unfortunate people who go around having loud conversations with themselves as there was no way of knowing he was in fact, giving me remote instructions as he stood on the stern deck, on how to dismantle the weed hatch while I sweated like a maniac in *Salamander's* sweltering bowels.

First, I had to undo a very tight, threaded handle, horizontally fixed across the top of the hatch and once this was free, I could undo the lid, which was surprisingly heavy. Inside the hatch was a steel rectangular piston which had to be lifted out, keeping it perfectly vertical; this was even more awkward than it sounded as there was barely enough headroom to manoeuvre it. Finally, I got my arms into the hole which had now appeared in the floor of the boat and I was surprised to see the water looked quite clean and was a lovely colour from the sunlight outside. Trying not to think too much about giant pike and catfish, I plunged my arms into the hole, groping around the propeller trying to locate the tangled rope. I shouted up to Ray that it was not in the propeller itself but was caught in a groove in the drive shaft and he shouted back to me that this was usually the case.

I had to come up for air; it was absolutely roasting down there. It was a hot day and the heat from the engine made it unbearable. Ray commented that I would need a sharp serrated knife or similar and since this tied in with the advice that Martin back in Watford had given me; 'Always make sure that you have a bread knife or similar to hand, because as sure as eggs is eggs, you will need it;' so I had one ready. After fifteen minutes or so I had made no impression whatever – it was certainly good rope. After coming up for more air, I swapped the knife for a tenon saw I had found lurking in a box and after another ten minutes the rope was finally severed. Ray passed more instructions down to me, this time reversing the procedure. He said a few times that he could have done the job for me but if he had, I would not have learnt anything myself. I nodded my head in agreement, giving it a good whack on the steel beam above me.

The crucial final act was to make sure everything was properly put back together with the rubber seals seated properly and tightened. When this was done, Ray switched on the engine and gave the throttle a gentle tweak, warning me to watch the weed hatch to ensure there was no ingestion of water, which there wasn't. A bit more power – still sound. I was happy – though stinking and dripping with sweat. Every cloud a silver lining (although I couldn't see how getting savaged by ginger dogs could have had a good outcome); I had learnt something essential for any boater to know – and now my centre rope was now exactly the right length.

I had heard bits of conversation while I was wrestling the rope but I was concentrating too hard to pay much attention. When I finally went upstairs I found Ray talking to an older man on a boat going the other way and they were both laughing. Ray told me that while I was broken down, the Aylesbury 'stealth boaters' had come up from our rear again but because of my mishap they were unable get through the lock and had to wait.

They complained bitterly to Ray about me, saying that 'that bloody' man' had been holding them up everywhere they went for the last two days, specifically mentioning the lock gates., Ray said that he had suggested that they might show a bit more compassion and understanding and that maybe people needed a bit of help sometimes but they weren't having any of it, insisting that I should be publicly flogged in Wendover market place until I saw the error of my ways. Ray suddenly remembered in fact that it was him who had left the last few gates open today and they suddenly changed their attitude.

'You can't let the one percent spoil it for the rest;' he told me, saying that he and the the recent arrivals were laughing because the new chap knew all about these four lovely people, who had gained a reputation in pretty nearly every boat yard across the southern canal network for their attitudes. Now doesn't that warm the cockles of your heart?

Ray only had to go around the next bend and he was at his destination so I shook his hand, thanking him most sincerely and we parted company. If I were an influential man I would recommend him for an MBE or maybe a knighthood for his services to boating. We had only shared each other's company for maybe two hours but in that time, he had made a huge impression – good Karma to you mate. He wouldn't be the last wonderful person I would encounter on this journey.

Looking behind me, I could see Ivanhoe Beacon disappearing into the distance and again, I felt sentiment for something I had for years considered fairly insignificant in my life, realising now that I might never see it again. I felt a rush of memories about my experiences in the Chiltern escarpment that I had grown quite fond of over nearly two decades.

I got to Leighton Buzzard by mid-afternoon and not knowing the best place to moor up, I ended up almost underneath a bridge. I desperately needed to buy some food and I could see there was a *Tesco* supermarket next to the bridge across the road. I was not too happy leaving *Salamander* there and asked some people on another boat if it would be OK, they said it would.

It was Friday, with heavy traffic and just like the previous time, I felt like Forrest Gump who had never seen cars before!

I eventually crossed the road but I still felt a bit uneasy about where the boat was parked and did my shopping in rush mode. Lots of people, hoping the good weather would continue over the weekend, were preparing to annoy their neighbours by stocking up with burgers, sausages, charcoal and the usual barbecue items that get wheeled out by the supermarkets at the end of March each year. In the military, there is a state known as 'hard routine', meaning that when in the field, under tactical conditions, whether on exercise or for real, it is forbidden to cook or light fires between dusk and dawn. The official reason naturally, is that any smoke, smell or light could give one's position away to the enemy but in the winter, when daylight is short, this can have a serious impact on morale (sapping morale is something the army is particularly good at anyway). An old buddy of mine after visiting my house on a few occasions and noticing the lack of biscuits and other non-essential junk food on offer, announced to the gathered crowds; 'Don't go to 'Farmer's' gaff especially in the winter – he's on permanent hard routine.' which of course, was received with much mirth and further mickey taking.

Be that as it may, I avoided all the barbecue items and finishing my shopping, decided to take a safer route back to the boat. I saw some signs pointing to the canal and followed them, eventually ending up on the towpath fully half a mile away from where I had started out but I arrived back finally at *Salamander* to find her safe and sound.

My main worry had been that since she was half hidden under the road bridge, it might have been seen by some as an invitation to drop large objects like paving slabs on to her (Observant readers may have noticed I have become influenced by nautical terms, referring to a boat as 'she' now rather than it) – I felt insecure too, because this was the first sizeable place I had stopped at since setting out. Even Hemel Hempstead, though more spread out, had seemed much quieter even though, it was a bigger town than this. Originally my intention was to stay the night here; despite the rope incident, I had made really good progress today thanks to Ray's assistance through the locks. So, looking at the map, I decided to push on to Soulbury only a few miles further on.

I have thought since that Leighton Buzzard might have been a good town to try a day's busking, I based this assumption on a very old painting of the town, depicting of all things, a street magician performing the traditional and ancient cups and balls trick. The really interesting thing about the painting was that the artist had also painted a pickpocket helping himself to the belongings of the unsuspecting audience, all of whom were leaning forward to get a better view of the trickery. The place had not changed much in some respects; I had seen a few dodgy-looking characters about that Friday. When I do perform my cups and balls trick, I usually mention the painting and the pickpocket in my patter and it is usually gets a laugh and it is fun to watch my spectators instantly checking their pockets and bags.

As I have mentioned previously, I thought the term marina was a slight exaggeration when referring to canals, so imagine my surprise when I saw a sign proclaiming, 'Welcome to The Wyvern Shipping Company!'

Recently I had had a conversation with a random stranger about the finer points of corned beef; the man told me he was a merchant seaman and his company specialised in the transportation of corned beef. He said their container ships would venture thousands of miles into Brazil's interior, all the way along the river systems.

Taking the shipping term a bit more seriously now, I slowed right down to a crawl as I went past the Wyvern Shipping entrance Instead of *MSC Oscar* embarking I only encounterd one of their hire narrow boats, crewed by three somewhat horsey looking women and a member of Wyvern Shipping Company staff. I gave way for them and he winked and thanked me for yielding, even though I officially had the right of way. I followed them as slowly as possible – boats are a bit like aeroplanes – they may be much slower but there is no pause button to press if things get too hectic – which can result in several boats all going in different directions and chaos ensues. The Wyvern chap interrupted his instructions now and thoughtfully waved me on past them before we reached the lock.

I noticed the canal here was becoming more river-like, as the canal guidebook said it would: the sun was now blazing, birds were singing and the canal twisted one way and back again. More and more green plants appeared on the bottom and it was hard to believe that I wasn't on a river. I was vigilant and ready to cut the throttle at any sign of this getting near the prop, I really didn't want to have to put my newly acquired mechanical knowledge to use again so soon!

The weather had changed by the time I got to Soulbury and it was now cloudy and much cooler; the most notable change being the rising strength of the wind.

I performed my by now, familiar routine; first make sure the (now shortened) centre line was to hand, along with a couple of mooring pins and a hammer, slow the boat right down, aim for the bank at a shallow angle and just before impact, give *Salamander* a little burst of reverse thrust. If I got it right, she would almost come to a halt right alongside the towpath and I could carefully step off on to the bank, rope in hand and bring her to a complete stop.

I did all this and took just a few seconds to bash the first pin into the ground but when I straightened up, I realised the front of the boat was rapidly drifting across towards the centre of the canal. I tried pulling but the wind had got a proper grip and only swung her further round. If I lost my hold now on the ever-shortening rope, *Salamander* would be gone forever – a bit like George Clooney floating off into space in the film *Gravity*. By taking a massive and risky stride, I was just able to get onto the very tip of the bow and regain my balance quickly before scrambling to a more secure position. What is it about us humans (maybe it's just the males) that whenever we are faced with danger or serious injury, our main concern is always 'I hope that no one saw that'? This was exactly what I was thinking now, on the stern deck at last and gunning the engine to regain control. *Salamander* was firmly glued to the bottom now (remember me saying that the average canal was about three inches deep!); I tried reverse and then hard forward but all this did was churn up tons of black mud around the propeller.

Changing tactics, I pulled the wooden barge pole hand over hand back along the roof until I could get a proper grip of it and pushed it into the canal floor, gently leaning all my weight onto it. Usually this would be enough to re-float her (yes, this wasn't the first time) but now the pole just got firmly stuck in the mud. I was starting to gather a small audience now and I was having visions of the boat suddenly moving on and leaving me stuck up a pole and stranded in the middle of the canal like something from a scene in a *Carry On* film, so I gave up the pole idea and tried the engine again with no luck

One of the bystanders who looked and sounded Spanish, shouted for me to throw him the rope. I did as he asked and he heaved and strained for a few seconds before losing interest and walking on, pressing buttons on his phone. A couple dressed in matching Faro sweaters said they too become stuck in the same spot once, and eventually had to be towed off by another boat. I was tempted to reply 'Well go and get your boat then' After what seemed like ages, they finally offered 'Would you like us to get our boat and give you a tow?' 'Oh yes please, if you would be so kind!' In the end, it only took a slight jolt before *Salamander* was afloat again and I could tie the bitch up to the bank correctly and begin my long evening of doing bugger all. There did not appear to be a lot going on here which was fine by me, the only disturbances being Virgin *Pendolino* trains, whooshing past at just below the speed of light every ten minutes or so.

Most evenings if I wanted to watch TV, the aerial would need re calibrating and since I had no idea which direction the signal would come from, I just relied on my built-in compass (which was usually surprisingly accurate). Some evenings I could get a massive selection of crap to keep me entertained, sometimes nothing at all but usually there were a dozen or so channels, BBC1, BBC2, ITV, etc. Interestingly, no matter how bad the signal, I could almost always get perfect Al Jazeera reception.

It amused me how quickly the TV regions changed and how irrelevant they often were to the particular area. I was now watching the local East Anglian BBC news but thirty miles to the south, I had been watching BBC South East. I don't think it will spoil the story, by jumping ahead saying that I did eventually get to my final destination.

Since arriving in Wales, the only BBC TV available is for the northwest region which is a huge area covering The Isle of Man, Cumbria (parts of which have been stolen from Yorkshire without our permission), Lancashire, Cheshire, Merseyside and Manchester. I have also seen a few items about the Peak District, parts of which are in South Yorkshire!

I can hear about how the IOM have finally agreed to allow gay marriage or how annoyed the tree-dwelling anarchists near Blackpool are because our caring government has agreed to let its mates start fracking and causing earthquakes again. I can watch and listen to all of this in my chosen bit of North East Wales but Chirk or Wrexham are not mentioned once. If a sink hole suddenly appeared five miles away in Llangollen and fifty black-woolled sheep fell down it, never to be seen again, I would be none the wiser. No wonder the Welsh have a problem with the English!

Chapter 5

Milton Keynes

I woke the next day (which I think was Saturday), to find the weather had reverted back to early March and looked just like it did when I set off last Tuesday. I dawdled around quite a bit, not relishing the thought of standing on the open deck in the cold wind and rain or the prospect of the Soulbury Three Locks just ahead of me, to get the day started.

I stepped onto the towpath ready to untie the boat when a lovely affectionate black dog suddenly came running up to me (if it had been the ginger ones from the other day, the vicious bastards would have taken me completely by surprise). Looking both ways along the path I could not see a soul – no boats – nothing. He was wearing a collar and was in good condition and after fussing around for a few minutes, he ran off as suddenly as he had appeared, I took this to be a good omen. Just as I was about to cast off, a couple of Scottish sounding women joggers with shaved heads went by and both wished me a good morning. .

My plan today was to make as much distance as possible around Milton Keynes, where because the town was flat, there would be no locks at all once I was north of Fenny Stratford. In fact, this would turn out to be one of the longest legs of the whole journey. The three locks ahead were soon reached and tying the boat up in the lock pound, I walked forward to assess the scene. A man in walking gear came over to have a chat and mentioned that he lived locally, was indeed a walker and he also owned a boat.

When we had finished talking, he offered to see me through the short flight, so that again, all I had to do was steer the boat and make sure that my baseball hat didn't blow away in the wind and rain. Among all the bits and pieces living in the engine room was one of those previously mentioned leather *Crocodile Dundee* hats, often worn by the worst type of boater (if my experience was anything to go by). I thought they were pretentious, exemplified by a man in Rickmansworth, who would turn up on his bike every day looking like a two-wheeled Ray Mears, wearing one of these hats and walking gaiters up to his knees. All this *I'm a Celebrity* jungle clobber was apparently necessary so he could sit in the local branch of a famous pub chain with a reputation for providing all-day drinking for a large group of men of a certain age. So mine would be staying where it was, on the hook, out of sight. I thanked the kind gentleman and off I went.

After about an hour I arrived at Fenny Stratford, which looked as if a bunch of civil engineers when they got here, had found that they had an embarrassment of materials left over from a monumental quantity surveyor's cock-up. In order to hide their mistake, they decided to build as many structures as possible. In the space of 150 yards there was a road bridge, two pipe bridges, a railway bridge, a swivelling footbridge, a lock and just to make the place look finished, a few canal-side buildings – and another pipe bridge. If all this wasn't enough, a road also followed the contour of the canal so closely, as to be almost a part of it. I was experiencing a bit of sensory overload here, there was so much to take in.

As I approached the swing bridge very slowly, two young girls were sitting on a bench watching me and as I was about to tie the boat up ready to operate the bridge, they both jumped up, asking excitedly if they could work the bridge for me. How lovely, I was tempted to say; you can work every bridge and lock from here to Llangollen if you like girls but then I thought about trapped fingers and the like. I didn't associate the man also sitting on the bench as being with them; thinking he looked too young to be their father but I said they certainly could swing the bridge for me, as long as an adult supervised them. They responded that the bench dweller was indeed their dad and he confirmed this with a nod, so off they went to do their duty. They told me they lived in one of the canal-side houses, pointing to it and apparently this was all they did, apart from the odd day off to go to school. I couldn't believe their enthusiasm but presumably they would start to lose interest when they discovered horses, boys or both. When I came to the next lock, they insisted on helping with that too, although I would not let them near the ratchets. So now I was free. There would be no more locks until I got to Cosgrove which would not be until Monday; I had decided that tomorrow would be a day of rest and I still had around nine miles to go today.

Milton Keynes seemed to go on forever; the canal circles, the city, everything looked just like the bit before and the next bit looked just the same. It was not unpleasant, just boring. Modern-looking concrete flats and houses almost in the canal – lots of trees -a road bridge – more concrete houses and flats another road bridge and more trees; it just went on and on. About halfway through this endless circumnavigation, I stopped to replenish my water tank and whiled away the time watching a group of youths on the opposite bank as they deliberately snapped and broke the branches off a tree. They then dumped a huge pile of rubbish next to the canal and went. They knew I was watching them but did they give a toss? It is not their fault, we are told. Bless 'em.

I was on my way again and just approaching the 765th bridge of the day when I caught a glimpse of two hire boats travelling in tandem, with what appeared to be an exclusive crew of females on the first one. I couldn't really see what was going on behind but there seemed to be a lot of arms aloft, screaming and whooping and general 'ladette' behaviour. As well, I could see they were travelling far too fast: I was a lot closer to the bridge than they were and unless I had got it all wrong, I had priority but sometimes discretion is the better part of valour (as my old Sergeant Major would say, usually just before he ripped some arrogant 2nd lieutenant to shreds).

They had no inkling of my approach or they just did not care, so I quickly slowed down and pulled over, bringing *Salamander* to an abrupt halt on the side. As the two boats came steaming under the bridge I got a better look; there were perhaps six or seven women on each boat they didn't see me at first. It was all a bit surreal; they were at the point of inebriation just before the nastiness begins like I say, miserable is often my default setting. When they eventually did see me, they went from a giggling, drunken, whooping gaggle to silence – instantly as one body; then groaned loudly and one of them with an expression on her face that would have turned milk sour said, 'Smile!' I didn't bother to reply but thought; All right – next time I'll just beam a huge inane grin, put my boat into full forward gear, and see what happens. like a wise old mate of mine once said; 'There's no point trying to argue with drunks and thickoes.' This lot were both. Grrr!

What with this and the fly-tipping tree-breaking episode, I decided I wasn't very keen on this part of the world and that I would do Milton Keynes in one go. I would get to the top side of it and find somewhere quieter to moor overnight and the next day. I hadn't noticed during all the excitement, that the sun had managed to make an appearance and it was now quite a nice afternoon. Because I wanted to see the end of concrete and bridges, I was pushing *Salamander* a little more than I have should have – not as fast as a lot of other canal users that I see but I was making a little bow wave every now and then. I started to feel a bit guilty and every half mile or so I eased off the throttle which not only preserved the canal banks (though to be fair they were concrete too), it also gave my hearing a rest as the engine was deafening at times.

What happened next was entirely my fault and still gives me a squirming, cringing feeling, as if the victims might still recognise me any time I dare to show my face in public. After going under yet another road bridge, there was a left-hand bend followed immediately by a turn to the right. At the apex of the first turn, sitting right under the bridge, I was expecting the canal to go straight on but rounding the bend, I saw there was a line of boats moored on the far bank much reducing the radius of the turn. I was going too fast – slowed down – and lost my steering. A well-timed gust of wind and I was travelling straight towards them, hitting one a glancing blow. I shouted an apology to the owner but he just looked at me and I was trying so hard to get around the bend and avoid the other boats that I didn't see what was coming next!

There was a little jetty leading from a pub garden jutting out into the canal right on the bend, with six or eight people sitting on it, drinking and enjoying the warm weather; a few of them even had their feet dangling in the water. The expressions on their faces were priceless and I suddenly had a vision of *Salamander* and me making the news headlines. Under pressure people do some unexpected things and I could see a few hapless souls were thinking; 'Should I just run, or have I got time to grab my bottle too?' Everything seemed to happen in slow motion; I put *Salamander* into full reverse and thankfully, almost stopped her just before impact. In my mind's eye, I was seeing a rerun of the scene in *Jaws*, where the two drunken rednecks tie a chunk of meat to the jetty, only for the shark to drag the whole jetty out to sea, or something like it. Instead, there was just a modest bump and a blur of scrambling limbs. Because of the wind and the impossible position of the boat, I had to get the barge pole off the roof again and push the boat backwards before I could rectify my course and continue. This was all done whilst I muttered a string of sincere apologies. I noticed that most of the escapees were drinking *Erdinger Weizen Beir*, a long-time favourite of mine so in between my apologies, I also attempted to pacify them by complimenting their impeccable taste in beer. By the time I had straightened myself and the boat out before resuming my killer journey, I noticed that quite a few residents of the line of moored vessels had now gathered, hands on hips to wish me a safe journey – or whatever.

On I voyaged, under more bridges, past more concrete flats and houses. To be fair, parts of Milton Keynes did look quite nice and I wondered idly where the concrete cows were but I never did see them. I remember years ago having a ridiculous argument with my then, nearly sister-in-law (that's another story) who was adamant that there could not possibly be such a thing as concrete cows in Milton Keynes or any other city for that matter. Her confident denial wasn't based on any contrary evidence or facts – just that she had been to university and therefore was always right. I believe she later became a social worker.

It was now late afternoon, almost evening and I had a sudden memory of childhood Saturday tea times. It was always the same thing for tea, week in and week out. Sticks of celery, pork pies and tomatoes that actually tasted of tomato. That familiar, rousing marching tune on the valve wireless (they weren't called radios in those days) just before they announced the football score. I never knew what it was called, and nor did anyone else I knew, although I would bet that my Grandad would have known. (It is called 'Out of the Blue', isn't Google wonderful?) I have no idea why I suddenly started thinking about events from fifty plus years ago then I came back to the present. The scenery had changed now and I had just entered a cutting with old factories and warehouses on either side.

Milton Keynes is always described as a new city but I realised that this was only relative as these buildings looked as though they had been here since the sixties. Of course, their original roles had changed and now they were fashionable flats and gyms. Two young women were sitting on a concrete and stainless-steel balcony about forty feet above the canal, drinking and looking discreetly down but pretending not to; far too precious to be concerned with mundane things like canals and no doubt wondering what it was making such a noise. I raised my hand, half in greeting and half apology but I should have known better – nothing – no acknowledgement – the invisible man on an invisible boat. I gave *Salamander* a vigorous burst of throttle, engulfing them and their Pimm's in acrid black diesel clag as I disappeared under yet another bridge.

Consulting my map, I liked the look of a place called Wolverton and decided to make that my destination for this evening.

Over the years, I have developed a facility for picking a spot on the map and based on nothing more than bird's eye representation and a 'funny feeling', I will arbitrarily decide if it feels right for me. Depending on what I was after, this often turned out to be surprisingly accurate…not always though!

At last, I seemed to have left the concrete of Milton Keynes behind and the canal-side began looking greener and more rural. While exercising my newly developed arse-rudder boat steering technique, I flicked through the last few pages of my canal guide and calculated the distance covered today and was pleasantly surprised to find I had navigated a full sixteen miles. There was a likely looking stretch of straight water ahead where a few boats were already moored. Following my now, routine docking procedure, I stepped off the boat onto the towpath. There was still quite a stiff breeze and instead of coming to a gentle stop, *Salamander* was now heading off towards the opposite bank.

For the first time I realised how tired I was, followed by a panicky thought – had I left the boat in gear? My mind flipped to a fleeting memory of being on the losing side of a tug of war; the acceptance of defeat, knowing all effort is futile Then I ran out of rope – and for the second time that week found myself catapulted backwards towards the ground. This time there was no grass – just horrible little stones.

Two little girls now appeared from out of nowhere; I had really hurt my elbow but I couldn't afford the luxury of grovelling about on the floor and got quickly back to my feet. One of the girls shouted that she would get her mum while her sister stood with her hand over her mouth, looking at the 'claret' dripping from my arm. Fortunately, the end of the mooring rope had not quite disappeared into the water. I managed to grab it again and with the other girl helping, we tried to tame *Salamander*. An intimidating looking shaven-headed, tattooed woman now appeared from a few boats further down; I don't think I have ever seen such a lean-ripped body before. 'Give me the rope;' she commanded – and I obeyed immediately. In moments, she had the boat completely under control and safely alongside, with all resistance gone. She looked at me now and said; 'Mooring pin!' That was when I realised I had left them, driven into the ground sixteen miles away, as well as the hammer. It was easier to just say I had lost them. Telling the two girls to 'Hold that,' she gave them the rope and ran to her boat, reappearing seconds later with two mooring pins and a B&Q hammer. My guardian angel then moored the boat safely and said I could keep the pins and might as well hang on to the hammer as well. I mentioned before that I was to encounter more wonderful people on my journey and these three certainly fitted that category. The girls, who I guessed were nine or ten years old, were both dressed in summery, flowered dresses, and their mum told me they were a family of six, all living somehow on a tiny plastic river cruiser – never judge a book by its cover! I told them about my voyage so far and where I was heading to, commenting that I would have to buy a new canal guide before long and the lovely woman promptly gave me an ancient looking map which conveniently covered the missing area. I tried inadequately to show my gratitude for their kind actions, so I did a few magic tricks for the girls, which made them squeal with delight. Then, looking forward to a day's rest, I did my nightly ritual study of my canal guide and felt quite pleased with myself. In five days, I had travelled forty-six miles and tackled fifty-six locks, most of them without mishap.

Wolverton though, proved to be a disappointment. It was miles to the nearest shops so I ended up buying a few essentials from one of those filling station-mini supermarket-type places; the sort where there is bugger all else for miles so they can charge what they like. There was a pub just up from where I moored, but I was too tired to go there anyway. It was another hot day and the canal was buzzing with activity. Returning to the mooring I noticed the boat was at a strange angle, different to how I had left her an hour or so earlier. On closer inspection, I saw that both mooring pins, though still attached to the ropes, were now in the canal. Luckily the boat hadn't drifted, possibly because the canal was so shallow but I suspected I might have had a visit from a few of the local 'chav' population. I bashed the pins back into a different patch of ground and re-tied the ropes but just has I finished, a hire boat screamed by at about 15 mph and ripped them out again. This pattern continued for the whole of the day and to ensure maximum misery, a dog barked loudly and ceaselessly from a nearby garden until around nine pm, which was also roughly when the endless stream of speeding boats began to dwindle. I couldn't wait for Monday to come around and I could say goodbye to the delights of Milton Keynes.

Chapter 6

Gayton

I was up and raring to go on Monday, very pleased to be getting away from Wolverton. I had not seen or heard from my rescue family but I could not just leave without seeing them again. I knocked on the side of their boat but there was no reply and I got the impression they had gone away or perhaps they had other family or friends living more conventionally nearby. I wrote them a sincere thank you note on the back of one of my business cards and pushed it through a gap in the hatch leading to the cabin. I wonder if they ever found it?

I set off with some anxiety, knowing this was probably the day I would have to go through Britain's third longest canal tunnel at Blisworth. It should be no big deal but it was a long one and I had not yet gone through a canal tunnel of any length. A few minutes later I navigated a right-hand bend under a road bridge and immediately found myself aloft the Great Ouse Aqueduct. It wasn't particularly spectacular, in fact it wasn't spectacular at all. It was however, different to the views I had experienced in the last few days and I was very grateful to whoever built it because the previous arrangement had meant going first up – and then down – eighteen locks – which would have entailed a fair few hours of intense grunting and straining. Just over the aqueduct, a sign informed me there was a water point and a holiday park with shop and due to yesterday's failed shopping spree, I was running on empty again. Shopping almost daily was a necessity because my only means of cold storage was a 12-volt mini-fridge about the size of a microwave oven. This marvellous piece of electronics dripped water constantly and made enough noise to rouse me from the deepest sleep when the thermostat kicked in at around two or three most mornings but at least it kept my pint of milk and packet of bacon cool.

I had a quick browse around the camp shop but it seemed to be owned by the same people who ran the local garage with prices at the same level of extortion. I bought the cheapest item I could see, a bag of stir-fry vegetables, reduced to 56p from £6.78. Mixed with some nine-month-old noodles and a tin of tuna I had been hoarding, this would have to do me for tonight. Why do producers insist on putting huge chunks of carrot which take about 15 mins to cook, in the same bag with shredded cabbage that cooks in 30 seconds? When I was training to become a chef, we were constantly reminded of the dimensions various cuts of vegetables must be. When the instructors felt bored or in a bad mood (most days), they would walk around our work areas, precisely measuring our production with a ruler. You soon learnt to whip your hands away if the Brunoise you had spent the last hour sculpting from a carrot wasn't exactly 1/8 x1/8 of an inch square. Also, no real chef was ever taught to use a knife like an out of control flail, like some TV chefs do just to impress their viewers. This precision was not just for presentation, or to satisfy the instructor's obsessive-compulsive disorder, it meant that things cooked at an even rate. My teachers would be spinning in their graves or care homes if they could see some of the standards that are accepted today.

After filling my water tank, off I went towards Northamptonshire. Contrary to my *Collins Nicholson* guide's information, there were no hills dominating the landscape to the west and nothing remarkable to see or do for the next few miles, until I reached Stoke Bruerne locks. This is a flight of seven locks, going uphill this time – my favoured direction – and the surrounding landscape was a wide-open space (a bit like Marsworth a few days ago but without the dogs). Just as I was cranking my way through the first lock, a man of about my age paused to watch, telling me in a Geordie accent that he quite fancied buying a boat. We then discussed keeping warm, wood burners and wood in general and by the time we had agreed on the optimum time needed to season pine, I was through the top gates, where he wished me well and continued walking his dog. Later (I can't remember if I caught him up or other way round), I was lucky enough to share the remainder of the flight with another boat whose owner was quite young and willing to do the lion's share of the work, telling me he was heading for Northampton. When I was planning this journey, I remember getting a shock when I discovered the approach to this town involved passing through over a dozen locks in quick succession. It makes you wonder...the Llangollen canal goes through over 40 miles of some of the most spectacular terrain in this beautiful land, and – wait for it – passes through a total of only 14 locks while the approach to a flat-ish Northampton looked more like the road to L'Alpe Duez. Looking at my proposed route again, much to my relief, I saw I didn't have to go that way but would turn off to the northwest at Gayton Junction. My new companion and I chatted for the next hour or so and went through the fifth lock together where he decided he would stop. (Coming into this lock, I hit the sidewall quite hard but did not think much of it, only discovering later the disaster this mishap was to cause). I thanked my friend for his help and set off alone towards the final two locks in the flight which as usual, were separated from the main flight.

The next lock was right beside a pub, complete with its complement of drinkers. Warping *Salamander* into the lock and closing the bottom gates, I walked to the far end and opened the paddles. While *Salamander* rose steadily to the top of the lock, I glanced across towards the pub expecting perhaps, a smile, comment or some pleasantry but was met instead with cold, expressionless stares. To save time and energy, I thought I could jump across the gap between the two gates which had already automatically opened half way, as sometimes happened. In the split second before take-off. a few related thoughts were going through my mind. First was Ray's story of falling into a lock and thinking that it must surely happen to me at some stage of this journey. I also recalled the time when an old colleague of mine once said before making a monumental culinary cock up; 'Why is it that you know something isn't right but you can't stop yourself doing it anyway?' I too, almost always get that premonition just as something goes wrong, knowing the Stanley knife you are using, pointing towards your hand, will slip under pressure, causing a painful injury – you know what is going to happen but still do it anyway. These premonitions are always too late to be of any use and so I leapt through the gap between the gates, instantly realising I was on a collision course with the one-inch square shaft where the windlass is usually attached – except this time it was still in my hand.

I have always hated dead legs, the school bully's best weapon – this was the ultimate example and the pain was outrageous. The steel shaft hit me right in the middle of the quadriceps; and I let go of the windlass which plopped loudly into the water, followed by my best and only fishing hat as I slumped in agony over the rail on top of the gate, not sure if I was about to faint or be sick. For a moment, I expected to fall into the lock myself, all the time feeling like a complete idiot. After twenty seconds or so, I began to recover my composure and sneaked a glance at the pub audience for any signs of a reaction but there was still nothing, just blank stares. By now I was doing a Native American rain dance shuffle like you do when in acute pain. I was not looking for attention but it was hard to believe that not one of the spectators had asked about my wellbeing. As if by magic, a woman appeared from nowhere, asking if I was alright. I got the impression she had some medical training, offering me loads of advice and asking if I had any anti-inflammatories. She must have been sitting there just waiting for this moment because next thing she pulled out a dozen *Nurofen* and gave them to me telling me that I could keep them. I was in enough pain to consider taking the whole lot in one go. To make matters worse, the scab on my elbow from the debacle during Saturday's docking in Wolverton had been torn off and was bleeding profusely again while my thigh had already seized almost solid. When I got a chance, I dropped my pants to inspect the damage, seriously considering the possibility that I might have ruptured the muscle but I was lucky, it was just badly bruised. So, for the next few days I would be hobbling around like the psychotic killer in *Magnum Force* after Clint Eastwood had discharged a couple of rounds into his thigh. The day was about to get even better soon!

The last lock of this flight was a couple of hundred yards ahead and I managed to get through it without maiming myself again, arriving at the much-anticipated village of Stoke Bruerne. To this day, I have no idea how to pronounce the second part of the name. This Stoke whatsits name looked really interesting, a very pretty village that tourists visiting England, I think should be forced to see along with so many other places off the beaten track, rather than the usual London, Bath and Stratford upon Avon.

The canal almost all the way up to the dreaded Blisworth tunnel was crowded with boats one of them sold food and drink – just what I needed. The owner and his wife were from Lancashire and travelled all over the place selling their goods – all home-made. He asked me what I was doing and then why I couldn't walk properly. When I told him and it must have done the trick because he threw in a free slice of the best-tasting cake I have had in ages. We chatted for about half an hour two more men came over to join in the conversation: one asked me where I was going and when I told them, he said he thought I should do it in about another four days from here. Chirk was still a good 140 miles away – his estimation would require me to travel an average of thirty-five miles per day -the most I had covered so far in one day was half that distance! His mate asked which way I intended to go and I said up the

North Oxford and the Trent and Mersey, keeping to the east and north of Birmingham. He asked me why I wanted to avoid Birmingham and I said that, amongst other reasons, I wanted to avoid the locks, to which he replied; 'There aren't any locks in Brum.' I thought to myself, well mate, according to my map, there are dozens – it showed so many black chevrons that it could have been mistaken for a knitting pattern, with dozens more on all the approaches to Britain's second city. But I didn't argue; my leg was throbbing and I was just too tired Why do these people come out with such things? They must know that they are talking nonsense and that people don't believe them. When I mentioned my anxiety about the forthcoming tunnel, the café man gave me advice on getting through it alive; apparently the best approach was to go through at a steady pace and not too slow. He also said under no circumstances panic and stop if you meet a boat coming the other way, which is just what most inexperienced boaters do apparently.

I made sure that *Salamander's* headlight was on and slowly approached the dreaded Blisworth Tunnel. A couple of people were standing by the entrance and as I arrived I asked them if the headlight was on; they affirmed that it was. Muttering something about forty minutes of terror, I vanished into the darkness and almost instantly saw a light coming the other way. Sure enough, the tunnel was built for two-way traffic – but only just – and only if both parties kept their nerve. I wasn't a 'go berserker' and had been in some fairly claustrophobic environments in the military but this was still pretty unpleasant. The boat felt as if it was going forwards at a constant 10% angle and any attempts to rectify this resulted in a bang as the boat hit the tunnel walls and the roof constantly dripped cold, smelly water. I knew there was adequate ventilation but by half way I could feel panic rising as the bore gradually filled with diesel exhaust. Estimating that I must be beyond the halfway point, I couldn't work out why the other boat was not coming close to me? After about twenty-five minutes I could clearly see the tunnel exit and realised this was what I had been looking at the whole time. There never was a boat coming the other way but because of the length of the tunnel, I had wrongly assumed it would not be possible to see the light coming from the other end. One of the most remarkable things about the whole experience was when I went into the tunnel, it was a beautiful sunny day and when I came out at the other end, the sky was grey and threatening. There was also a smell – very similar to aviation fuel – coming from inside the engine compartment.

Once I was clear of the tunnel I moored up, deeply suspicious to know what was making the Heathrow Airport smell. Ducking down into the bilge, my suspicions were confirmed. One of the tins of emerald green paint had fallen off the shelf which must have happened when I hit the side of the lock earlier. Sod's law meant the entire contents were now sloshing around in the bottom of the boat. The prop shaft was now green along with most of the sides of the bilge.

When I bought *Salamander*, one of the first things to catch my attention was that there was not a drop of water in the bilge, it was bone dry. Of course, this was largely because it had not moved in years but now, after over a week of cruising, the inevitable had happened and there was now a fair amount of water in there, doing its best to mix with the paint. My heart sank. I was dog tired, my leg would hardly bend and I was cold and hungry but before I could deal with any of these issues, I would somehow have to remove the paint.

Gayton Junction was busy with boats everywhere so I went on round the bend to the left. I was now in open countryside and easily found a space away from the few other boats there. This was only five miles from Northampton but it was very peaceful, the only disturbance being a distant whoosh and rumble as the trains on the West Coast Mainline flew by about every ten minutes. I made myself a brew and got to work. Luckily, I had two of those cheap, last-about-a-week mops that look like the hair on a cabbage patch doll. These would be sacrificed and I just hoped there was enough absorption between the two, to soak up all the paint and water. After twenty minutes of swearing, sweating and banging my head, most of the grunge was soaked up, I put the first mop into a black bin bag after squeezing the contents back into the tin. Using the second mop as a makeshift brush, I painted the sides of the bilge with the leftover paint. There was still a fair bit of paint on the floor but I hoped the heat of the engine would dry it out eventually (No such luck!). Even though I had taken the precaution of wearing gloves, somehow, I still managed to get a lot of paint on my hands. I was not sure what kind of paint this was but paint thinner just spread it more evenly over my hands and almost up to my elbows, so that I now looked like the unfriendly witch in 'Wicked' and this was how I would continue to look for the next two weeks.

Chapter 7

Braunston and Rugby

Looking out of the window I could see that summer had taken yet another break. It was cold, grey and windy again and I was feeling exhausted – the sort of tiredness that drags on, even after a good night's sleep. This journey was starting to feel like a water-borne *Tour de France*, only instead of the Alps and Pyreneans, the relentless locks felt like the mountains to be faced each day with never a chance to recover. I was starting to forget which day was which. Still, at last, this was the day I would finally get to see the legendary Braunston. After all these years, I would see for myself exactly where and what it was. Today would be a flattish stage of around nine and a half miles until the I reached the first locks at Buckby. I had a quick look in the bilge, hoping that somehow the paint would have dried miraculously overnight but of course it hadn't. The inch or so still on the floor had now grown a skin – so that was it – I would just leave it to set and perhaps (in another eleven years or so) I could simply lift it out, roll it up and pop it into the bin.

The first three locks at Buckby were fairly straightforward, except that I managed to drop another windlass into the canal. A kind lady who had just exited the lock, saw what I had done and asked me if it was the only one I had. Guessing she was perhaps about to offer me a replacement, I reassured her I had lots more – one in fact. A quick calculation showed that in the last week and a bit – around seventy miles – I had shed half a top rope, the hot water heater flue (although I retrieved that and it was now balanced precariously on the roof), two windlasses, at least four mooring pins, a few hammers and one fishing hat. Oh – and the half tennis balls I had thoughtfully placed as a warning atop the mooring pins were also missing in action.

When I got to the fourth lock, I saw that the builders had thoughtfully introduced a little footbridge, bisecting the steps at the entrance to the lock chamber which meant that the smooth fluid motions of walking up the steps calmly with top rope in hand, would now be interrupted by having to thread the rope under the obstacle. Nothing too major but it had to be taken into consideration – several tons of floating steel cannot be stopped instantly. This arrangement was not just a one-off either, it featured on every lock for the rest of the day.

Although I have always considered myself to be a reasonable map-reader. I found myself having to consult my *Collins Nicholson Waterways Guide* with increasing frequency. There were two reasons for this; in the first few days of the journey, junctions were a rare novelty but now they were appearing more often and I needed to keep abreast of them as one wrong turn could mean a large waste of canal miles. For the uninitiated (I hope this includes most of you), you cannot just do a three-point turn anywhere on a canal – you have to find a designated turning point. The second reason for checking my route every mile or so, was that I appeared to be suffering from some kind of 'Cartogrylexier' (I just invented that word) syndrome – was it me – or were these canal map guides particularly confusing?

Let me try to explain. The pages don't always go in logical sequence, so it is quite easy whilst arse-steering, to turn a page expecting to be on the next section of the Grand Union Canal but instead of heading north, I would be looking at a completely different canal, which was now taking me south towards Oxford, or up the River Lea Navigation in Essex. It doesn't help that the maps are of such a large scale, so that the surrounding features aren't shown and it is difficult to get any to reference the immediate surroundings; it just shows a canal in the middle of a white page and more to the point, when I turned the page, I never knew if the direction of travel would appear at the top or the bottom. I was knackered too but checking for the umpteenth time, I decided that when I got to Norton Junction, my route should swing off to the west.

Another hour and I was approaching Braunston Tunnel which almost took me by surprise. After all the anticipation of yesterday's subterranean adventure, I had quite overlooked this forthcoming feature. Braunston Tunnel was around 1000 yards shorter than Blisworth, but still quite substantive enough to give me a few butterflies and this time, there really was a boat coming towards me. When entering a dark space on a boat, the mind immediately plays games and as I got closer, I could not be quite sure but it looked like the other boat had stopped and was jammed at an angle across the tunnel. I could hear a female voice shouting what sounded like 'Stop! Stop!' but I had no idea if she was shouting at me or the person driving her boat. As I said, the last thing to do is stop, so I ploughed on not knowing what to expect. By the time I got there, they appeared to have sorted themselves out and were going in a straight line and we passed each other with inches to spare. I could see the woman's face glowing like a Halloween lantern in the light reflected off the wet tunnel walls. She said something to me which sounded very much like 'Twat' as we passed each other but the combined sound of both engines drowned her words and they were gone.

When I finally got to Braunston, it was everything I had imagined. A real little canal city with locks, bridges, marinas, workshops – and lots of moored boats. So many boats that I could not find a single space to leave mine, so I chugged slowly past the endless lines, watching the bustling canal infrastructure pass by. I went around a right-hand bend, aptly named Braunston Turn but still had to go several hundred yards more before I found an empty space. At last, I was on a different canal – this was the Oxford Canal. Consulting the guide yet again, I saw that the actual village of Braunston was close by, just over the bridge, up a hill and along a public footpath. But this would have to wait until morning – the Milton Keynes day had been my longest until now but today had been almost as long – together with fourteen locks and I was knackered. The weather had got worse and it was cold and grey – unbelievable conditions even by British Summer standards. (Later that year I read that the temperature on Christmas Day was higher than this today, the 8th June) After going through the daily TV aerial fiddling ritual and finding absolutely nothing, confirming that Braunston was really on the dark side of the moon, I got the fire roaring, had a meal of which I recall nothing and was fast asleep by around nine pm.

Next day was still cold and blustery. I neither knew, nor was I much bothered about my destination for today, my first priority was to go shopping. I walked onto the top of the bridge that spanned the canal and cheered up slightly to see that for the first time since arriving here, I could get a phone signal. Before leaving Watford, I had initiated the process of cashing in an ISA, thinking that the money might come in handy. There were voice mails from *Scottish Widows* urging me to contact them but that would have to wait; no doubt it would consume my entire month's data allowance waiting for a connection to the relevant department, so for now, I would file them into my subconscious along with all the other stress triggers.

Braunston turned out to be a pretty little village with one pub, a couple of shops and a garage. I bought a few food essentials for an outrageous price and most importantly, a bag of logs for the fire. I carried all this back to the boat and dumped it, then picked up the jerry can and was about to return to the village when I had second thoughts and decided to wait until I got to my next destination, probably Rugby, where there must be a petrol station. I had a little sack trolley thing left over from my mobile DJ-ing days, that was really useful for humping things like sacks of coal and petrol cans but because the route to the garage was mainly off road along a rough track, it would not have been much use in this instance. I didn't fancy carrying it either.

When I was in the Territorial Army, a mate and I (the one that ribbed me about the lack of biscuits at my house) once took it in turns to carry a jerry can full of water for about two miles, on our way to a day's shooting on the range. The *Bravo Two Zero* book was doing the rounds at the time and in it, the alleged author Andy MacNab, mentioned that patrol members had to hump a jerry can full of their own body waste everywhere, so as not to leave any clues for the enemy. There were about twelve members in our group and we carried the thing between just the two of us, for a laugh and to see how difficult it would be -and it was difficult – this is the humor and mentality of the average British soldier.

Today I wore two thermal shirts, a fishing jacket and gloves and would have worn my hat too, if it had not been lying at the bottom of a lock. The canal was much narrower here, no longer wide beam like the Grand Union and I had only gone a few miles when I saw that the stretch of water ahead had a line of boats, double parked all the way as far as the eye could see. Coming down the centre towards me I could just make out another boat, instinctively I slowed right down to a crawl peering into the distance but could not judge if there was enough room for two boats to squeeze through without collision, so I slowed some more. A gust of wind caught the boat suddenly, blowing her across the canal and I lost all control. I looked behind to see that I was being tailgated by another vessel and next thing, he was overtaking me. As he came alongside he shouted, 'Why have you stopped?' at me, in his best 'Etonian.' I shouted back to him 'Because I thought there was not enough room to get two boats through the channel.' 'Well of course there is, you bloody fool.' he snarled, pushing past me at the same time. A red mist descended and for a second, I considered stepping onto his deck and delivering a swift head butt. Instead I shouted, 'Oi **** unlike you, some of us weren't born experts, we have to learn to do things through experience.' He heard me but just roared off. Oh yes – he too was wearing dungarees and a *Crocodile Dundee* hat – was there a pattern emerging here? I went on my way, seething for the next hour or so and hoped I might encounter him again later, on dry land and have the opportunity to debrief him properly.

I now began to flap about how much diesel I had in reserve and where I could get some. I cursed to myself for not thinking about refuelling until now. The fuel intake was just next to my foot so I got out my special 50p and undid the lid, at the same time trying but failing to keep the boat in a straight line. I could not see what the exact quantity was, only that it was definitely not full now. I flapped some more, thinking about what I would do or who I could phone if the engine suddenly spluttered and stopped. I did not have a clue so I forced myself to think about something else instead. There were no locks so far and I cheered up slightly on seeing the outskirts of Rugby getting closer. I saw a sign for a marina and a wave of relief swept over me – yes – I could get some diesel. The marina was on the opposite side of the canal so I didn't need to go inside to get to the fuel, thanks to a thoughtfully placed little canal-side jetty. It was very short though, and I could see it would take some precise docking if I wasn't to look like an idiot. (yet again!) If I got it wrong and the boat did not stop completely, there would be no room to run alongside; I would run out of space and end up in the water. I conjured up images of WW1 biplanes making spectacular cock-ups landing on the decks of aircraft carriers and flopping into the sea.

In the end, the jetty was in fact, a bit longer than it had seemed at first; I took it very slowly and no drama ensued. I went inside the office with the anxiety of running out of fuel now being replaced by the hope that my debit card would work. Ever since I had a payment declined (years ago) in a petrol station for no obvious reason, the nagging fear returns when filling up my car – or my boat. The man at the desk told me to go and fill her up, 'It's OK, I'll trust you.' I let the Diesel flow until the tank looked quite full and went back inside to pay. 'Would you like it 40/60?' The friendly man asked. 'Sorry, I...?' Before I could finish, he repeated the question '40% – 60%?' 'Well no I want it all.' He gave me a sympathetic smile and said 'No mate, for tax reasons, you have to state if it's for propulsion or for heating etc. So – 40/60 – all right?' 'Uh yeah, I suppose so.' I was delighted when the payment accepted sign appeared after a few seconds and asked if they sold petrol too but no luck.

Proceeding on my way, I now went under another bizarre structural arrangement; a skewed road bridge with the road, immediately it had crossed over, running perfectly parallel to the canal before ducking under two railway bridges, side by side, at 90% to the road and just to finish things off, the whole complex was situated on a huge bend. Once I emerged safely from under all this, I saw a familiar sight; dozens of massive transmission masts and support cables. I had often seen this sight from the M1 on my frequent car journeys from north to south, but never knew what they were all for. Must *Google* it one day.

After about 3/4 of a mile I arrived at Hillmorton Locks, there was something odd about these. After a few seconds, I realised what it was. These were only one boat wide, rather than the double arrangement I had got used to and I breezed through them all, feeling so much easier now. Another two miles and I found a likely looking place to moor up for the night. I was now in the suburbs of Rugby, it was still only mid-afternoon and the sun had made an appearance. Things were looking up! I had a shower, found the jerry can and trolley and set off to find a Tesco, asking directions from a couple with a broad West Midlands accent. They gave me vague instructions but I didn't really understand them; not because of their accent, I just couldn't make any sense of what they told me. I must have walked a mile along the towpath with the empty jerry can rattling and pinging at every bump in the track before realising I had no idea where I was going. Some young lads were sitting on the far side of the canal watching me, probably trying to figure out why I had green hands. I asked them where Tesco was and they told me it was in the other direction, up and over the bridge.

I was close to the centre of Rugby now and could see the railway station in front of me, I instinctively knew this was not right; I did an about-turn and retraced my steps, setting off back in the direction from which I had just walked, the rattling of the can on the trolley was becoming an irritation. A young woman was walking towards me and when she got within spitting distance, I asked her if she knew where Tesco was but she neatly side-stepped me with a pained expression. I was quite shocked by this reaction; I had asked her politely enough and despite my 'Wurzel Gummage' appearance, I thought there was no need for that. Even in the heart of London I had never faced such a rejection, when asking for directions or for anything else.

I was once almost knocked out by a man in a tube station who caught me a glancing blow running for his train and was surprised when about six people came to my rescue as I staggered about on jelly legs, asking if I was all right. Just don't get into difficulties in Rugby though. In the end, I walked all the way back to the boat where I saw a different path leading away at right angles to the canal. I walked up this – and there it was – Tesco.

Mind you, it was still quite a walk to the petrol area; these places were not designed for pedestrian access, so I was playing dodge the car again. I am not sure why I felt I needed permission but I asked the woman in the bulletproof kiosk if it was all right to fill the jerry can, which she said was OK. I cannot quite remember what the problem was but I just could not get the pump to work. The woman shouted helpful advice from her window but I still could not get anything to flow out of the spout. Finally, after several minutes I managed to fill the can and when I went over to pay, she was laughing. I said something about what a palaver – it was as if I had never used a petrol pump before. She misunderstood me, thinking I really had never used one and looked quite startled; 'Oh, haven't you?' I quickly cleared up the misunderstanding; the last thing I wanted was her telling all her mates; 'I had this bloke here today – must have been fifty if he was a day – he reckoned he had never used a petrol pump before until now – Fancy that eh? He had weird green hands too – I bet he lived with his mum.' I went off whistling, knowing I would have electricity tonight but I would still have to come back again to buy food; I couldn't really wander around the Deli Counter pulling twenty litres of petrol behind me.

Chapter 8

Hawkesbury Junction and Other Grim Places

Rugby had not endeared itself to me but there again, like most of the places I passed through, I had not really seen the town itself – just a supermarket, a distant railway station, loads of building under construction and a particularly unpleasant woman. (I still call the place where trains stop, a railway station, rather than the more PC and dumbed down, 'train' station. When I was at school we would have had a whack across the knuckles with a ruler for saying such gibberish as train station, and then another one for saying ruler and not rule.)

I was seven the last time I went to Rugby, which before the M1 was built, was a full day's journey from Yorkshire in the early 1960s. Someone from my dad's huge family was getting married but I cannot remember now who it was. There were thirteen other offspring in my dad's family, who will have naturally reproduced into what could now be thousands of relatives and I have no idea where any of them are!

My intended destination today was the rather grand-sounding Hawkesbury Junction: again, quite a long twelve mile stretch but I was not too concerned now because there were no locks until the very last bit at the junction itself and the sun was now shining again, making the surrounding landscape look wonderfully lush and green after the last days of grey and wet gloom.

The canal guide told me about the Newbold-on-Avon tunnel but it still took me by surprise. I was enjoying the sunlit landscape and almost forgot to turn on the headlamp ready to go through. It wouldn't have been the end of the world if I had, Newbold tunnel was a mere 250 yards, nothing like the terror of Blisworth or Braunston (which I imagine would be quite difficult to say over and over after a few pints). The guide mentions that the tunnel was built during the shortening of the Oxford canal, taking out a lot of unnecessary bends and making a more direct route.

An unfortunate by-product of the sunshine was that the canal was now very busy and everyone was in a hurry and I found myself having to yield to boats at just about every bridge, regardless of whether I had priority or no. Not a major problem but an occasional thank you would have been nice. For the benefit of landlubbers, the channel under all canal bridges narrows to the absolute minimum width, presumably to cut down on the amount of materials used which would have been quite significant – there are a lot of bridges out there on the canal network.

For the next few miles I was in a long day-dream, thinking about random things – would people still have dogs if there were no canal towpaths – wondering what the total UK duck population was and what was the point of signs showing a fish with a diagonal red stripe through it – could the fish even read them? I was abruptly brought back to reality by the M6 Motorway, crossing over the water on a huge concrete bridge. The West Coast Railway line was also back, running alongside the canal again just as it had for most of the journey. All the noise and speed felt completely alien now,

The green fields became fewer and the surroundings more urban. Council houses (or what had been) appeared in their thousands, all grey and pebble-dashed with allotments spreading almost to the canal's edge. The other bank was even more depressing; lots of electricity pylons with cables radiating from huge substations and going in all directions. A vast and sprawling site with no humans to be seen. The transformers and cables were emitting low frequency hums and hisses and the whole thing made my skin crawl. I shuddered and made the boat go a bit faster but it still took a good five minutes to get past. I may not have been there but I imagined this might be what Chernobyl would look like. People who protest about a few wind turbines ought to come and have a look at this lot.

Not long after, I was standing beside *Salamander,* scratching my head and wondering why anyone would deliberately build a lock with a depth of only six inches. I now know it was a stop lock, built to maintain the equilibrium, usually when two canals meet or to stop one canal company stealing the other's water. At the time though, I was convinced it had been put here just as an annoyance factor, something to keep boaters paying attention, after the dreary endless miles. This was Hawkesbury Junction and as well as the mini lock and several footbridges crossing here and there, I was required to do a complete 180% turn here, which involved manoeuvring round two 90% turns in quick succession with, of course, a thoughtfully situated pub next to the first turn, complete with the obligatory crowd of afternoon drinkers sitting at tables outside as my witnesses.

I probably could do all this fairly easily now but back then it seemed pretty difficult; I had to make a couple of attempts at getting round the first bend and then went far too wide on the second, having to reverse and try again, this time avoiding the overhanging bushes, I remember thinking; 'If watching boats from pub gardens is your hobby – good – if you have some useful comment or helpful tips, let me hear them – but please do not just sit there mumbling and moaning about my lack of skill to your drinking buddies. I would not go into their bedrooms and give a commentary on their performances. I looked online later hoping for conformation that Hawkesbury Junction was indeed a bit of a challenge to get around and was pleased to read that lots of other boaters had experienced traumas here. Someone had thoughtfully posted a link to a YouTube clip which showed a boat only slightly shorter than the warship *HMS Queen Elizabeth,* towing an un-powered vessel of a similar size around this inverted football goal-shaped junction but they got through first time without even touching the sides – so there you are.

I have absolutely no recollection of where I moored that evening which must have been a combination of chronic fatigue combined with the dreary suburbs of Coventry. Consulting my captain's log for that day, it just says; Stopped at Hawkesbury junction, then in brackets, (just up from there); which would have been Bedworth. I mention I was almost turned to stone by a grumpy angler when I greeted him and commented too that people are now speaking with a broad Midlands accent. Strangely on the next line,

I note that people's attitudes were changing for the better and they were generally becoming more friendly – except for worm drowners! This regional accent thing has always fascinated me. I can often establish quite accurately where a person comes from after listening to a few sentences. I absolutely astonished a fellow soldier once, shortly after just becoming acquainted. I was able to tell him which town he came from in Norfolk (although I was guessing a bit). For years I have pondered whether accents change gradually from north to south and left to right, or if there is a virtual line somewhere on the A1 where people talk about; 'Cor blimey, apples and pears' and walk with an exaggerated swagger on one side while just a few feet further north, they whistle for their pet whippet and speak broad Yorkshire.

I must have been in bed again by nine and that was Hawkesbury Junction and Bedworth. I was on the Coventry Canal now and felt I was really making progress. More importantly, I was about to run out of *Collins and Mitchell Waterways Guide 1*. In pencil at the top of the last page, I had written 97 miles, 89 locks and above this was printed – *See book 3*. I didn't have a book 3 but if you remember, the Amazonian like women at Wolverton, had given me an ancient looking map which was now to be my sole means of navigation for quite a few days. I had only glanced at it before but on closer inspection, the thing looked hand drawn and to be able to read any of its vital information would require the combined power of both my strongest Poundland glasses and a magnifying glass.

It also contained such important information as half -day closing along the way, something I had completely forgotten ever happened. I have no idea when this was phased out but for the information of anyone under thirty, I can tell you that this involved, unbelievably, the official closure of all shops in every town and village for one half day a week. And to make it even more confusing, the day would change from one place to the next.

These days were marked on the map so that any strangers about to visit Little Haywood wouldn't get their half day off confused with Great Haywood's half day of skiving and find that they couldn't buy any lard or fresh herrings for tea. I would not have been surprised to find it also told where pirate treasure was buried. However, the really vital statistics were still valid; canal courses and locks do not change much over the years and this chart would save me about sixteen quid by not having to buy another official guide which I would only be using once.

I say use once, I have been caught out a few times on frequent returns to the south by having binned maps covering places I thought I would never see again, only to have to buy a replacement a few years later. Strange – I have no problem hoarding just about every other item or piece of junk, just in case. Before the Internet ruined all our lives, I bought monthly editions of the most popular magazine for every hobby I indulged in – running, cycling, triathlon, railways, art, photography, DJ and music, flight simulation, science and loads of other things, some of them now long forgotten. I have weaned myself off almost all of the publications in recent years but I did crack once a few months ago when I bought a fly-fishing magazine, but only because they were giving away a DVD that actually had something about fishing on it. The rest of the issue was mainly adverts that only cost £5.99 for the privilege of reading. It's strange though, these days the racks in WH Smiths seem to display more crap than ever.

The scenery (or lack of it) continued just like yesterday; housing estates, pylons, allotments, motorways and bridges. The only thing of any real interest was the now fast approaching Atherstone lock flight and I had the familiar anxious feeling, not quite knowing what to expect. Being Friday afternoon, I thought it would be busy but I was the only boat there (maybe it was half day closing) and better still, there was a team of Canal and River Trust volunteers to help me negotiate the locks.

I said to one that I desperately needed to do some shopping before going up the flight and he showed me where I could moor, saying there would be no problem as long as another boat didn't arrive. This put me under instant pressure and I set off, taking big strides along the road bridge straddling the canal, guessing that Atherstone was off to the right, which it was. The town or village, looked like it's best times had been and gone. It reminded me of somewhere in urban South Yorkshire...in the 1970's! I went into the first shop I saw, got my bits and pieces and set off back to the boat, having a little internal flap in case it had vanished into thin air or thirty other vessels had suddenly manifested from nowhere and were all waiting for me to get out of the way.

When I arrived back, *Salamander* was still the only boat there and the volunteers said I could stay on the boat while they operated the locks for me. They stressed a few times what a huge favour they were bestowing on me and I showed suitable gratitude when the summit was reached. Just as I cleared the top lock, another boat came up behind me and

I forget what question I asked but the other volunteer said that the man on this boat would know the answer because he was the canal padre. I had no idea that such things existed and indeed he did know the answer to my query. He told me he just cruised up and down the same stretch of water, eternally looking for people that needed blessing. I wonder if they have padres dedicated to motorways too? I once waited on the freezing hard shoulder of the M40 for hours, courtesy of a VW ignition coil a padre could have been quite useful, although a St Bernard dog would have probably been more appropriate.

Another hour or so of cruising and I was at Polesworth, just to the south east of Tamworth. I was back in open countryside again now and decided to call it a day; besides it had started to rain. For the first time since leaving Watford, there was no traffic noise – I strained an ear – nothing. There was no-one else moored here and I was on my own. For safety reasons people told me never to moor alone but tonight I would take a chance. I did my nightly TV tuning ritual but got nothing except Al Jazeera. There was no mobile phone signal either so if someone wanted to be rid of me, this would be a good night to try; I was too tired anyway to put up much resistance. After eating whatever would fit into one pan, I had a shower and got the 'Genny' going. At least I could get reception on my mobile Internet dongle, so I would not have to twiddle my thumbs and stare at the wood cladding all night long.

Chapter 9

Amington

I slept for the best part of ten hours that night. The next morning it was bucketing down but it didn't matter – it was Saturday again – my day of rest and I lazed around doing nothing until mid-morning. I knew the boat needed cleaning and tidying up but finding the motivation to do anything was a problem; apart from the omnipresent railway line, the place was so tranquil. Train sounds have never bothered me in the least but I noticed the trains flying past here made a very strange sound. Instead of the familiar Doppler effect when a train approaches and then fades away when it passes, the sound was different here; the approach build-up was normal but then the noise would stop instantly, as if someone had unplugged the overhead power supply. After puzzling about this through for most of the night and next morning, I concluded there must be a tunnel nearby. It sounded quite eerie and made me shudder a bit each time. For some bizarre reason just looking at a river or a tunnel on a map always gives me a strange disturbed feeling. Perhaps I have real untapped powers of divination!

I went into one of my usual daydreams, this time on the arguments for and against the new 'HS2' scheme the Tory government is adamant about building. If it means losing your house, I can understand the distress but getting all worked up because the new line may come near your Buckinghamshire village is surely different; in my view a train whooshing by every 20 minutes is not really any hardship, what really hacks me off is the ever-increasing noise of cars and motorbikes being driven at 120mph in what sounds like second gear.

In the time, it took me to write the last few paragraphs down, three south bound trains had gone by and I remembered an MP talking about the housing crisis, saying we cannot all live in the southeast. I had no idea why they would want to but from the imbalance of south to northbound trains, he may have been right. Perhaps Stafford was just a horrible place and lots of people were desperately trying to escape to a better life in the south. Another Virgin Pendolino raced past, hitting the invisible wall and falling silent. It had taken me almost two weeks to get here while the passengers on the train could be drinking flat beer in London at £5 a pint in less than an hour (if that was their choice). In the meantime, I would still be here wondering what to do with myself.

The rain stopped around 1pm and as I didn't fancy staying here until tomorrow with no communications, I looked at my ancient chart and saw that Amington, at the top end of Tamworth, was within striking distance. I had a quick tidy around, got the engine chugging and set off towards Amington. The rain started again but I had anticipated it and was already wearing the fishing waterproofs. The canal here was dead straight and a bit boring; the inevitable man and dog appeared and I could see him eyeing me with suspicion, perhaps because of my boiler suit, tree patterned jacket and green hands which now had the appearance of faded do-it-yourself tattoos (the sort that people in Borstal might have worn, back in the days when we still had such deterrents). When he got level with me, I eased the engine so I could hear better and asked him about Amington. This seemed to put him at ease and he told me I could find everything I required there and recommended a pub, the name of which, I instantly forgot. I thanked him and chugged on in the pouring rain.

The canal went right through the middle of the village which made me feel a bit uneasy, particularly because I could not see any other boats anywhere and the place looked like it was mainly populated with my favourite type of people – 'chavs'! I checked that my impromptu pepper spray, also known as *Deep Heat,* was in its place under my pillow (just in case, with the increasing aches and pains). It was already around seven and since I was too tired to cook, I thought I would treat myself to fish and chips. I didn't have to limp far to find what I was looking for but though I have had some bad fish and chips in my time, these were the worst I had had in decades. I ate what I could and binned the rest, wondering how someone could make such a 'cock-up' of something so simple. Walking back to the boat, I noticed a young woman typing away in a bedroom window and wondered what she might be writing.

I was determined to go out for a few pints tonight – my first run ashore since Watford – unbelievable. I walked past the 'world's worst chippy' again, which was now closed, preventing me from being tempted to indulge in another bag of grease on my way back. I had no idea where I was going but the buildings were more plentiful in this direction and arriving at a crossroad, I saw what looked like a watering hole. The building looked quite odd; I could see it had not been a pub originally but before I got through the door, I could also see it had no character at all (perhaps it had first been used for a doctor's surgery?).

Taking a deep breath, I ventured inside, where three things were immediately apparent; the place was sweltering, the music was deafening and other than the server, there were no women to be seen. I have not liked drinking in exclusively male company since my Army days; I may have few ambitious ideas nowadays when it comes to attracting the opposite sex but I think most men would agree it is still nice to window shop and enjoy a bit of female company now and then.

There is an infamous pub called *The Trafalgar* in Aldershot (I always thought the title would have been more appropriate in Portsmouth or Plymouth). It was not the worst, that distinction belonged to the *Royal Military*, universally known as the 'Rat Pit' (This was the pub that the desperate or insane would choose when looking for a good scrap). The *'Traf'* was patronised by members of the airborne forces – this was not optional – if you weren't a member of one of the parachute units, you didn't go in there – unless you had a death wish. Because I was attached to '3 Para', I was allowed and tolerated, which was all very kind of the lads but the place was dire and women simply didn't go in there. It was the sort of place where bored Paratroopers took it in turn stapling beer mats to each other's foreheads! For two years I must have spent most evenings in there before rebelling and refusing to go out at all unless we went somewhere else. A few of the lads agreed with me but most of them thought the *'Traf'* was Nirvana.

So, as you can imagine, I was now having a bit of a flash-back in this Staffordshire dump. Rather than Levi 501 jeans and maroon tea shirts (the off-duty uniform of the discerning paratrooper), all the men were wearing vests and I couldn't really blame them, it was stifling. I eventually attracted the barmaid's attention and asked for a pint of Carling. 'Paardern?' 'A pint of Carling please,' this time she understood me. 'That's threow pound twenty, duck.' I took my pint and assumed the position with my back to the bar. Since getting involved in the wonderful world of magic, I always carry a few magic bits and pieces in my pockets, which may well not be used but it only takes a chance conversation and once people discover they are in the company of 'Merlin', they usually want to see something. I thought about them now but knew they would be staying put; entertaining the locals in here tonight was not looking very likely. A huge YouTube video projection of Diana Ross singing *Chain Reaction* was showing on the far wall and I watched it mesmerized, for a few minutes. If the deafening volume of the music wasn't enough, the words were also thoughtfully subtitled...in Spanish! I asked my vest-wearing, foot-tapping neighbour why this was but he completely ignored me. By the time he did eventually respond, I was already putting my jacket on ready to leave and missed his reply. I finished the rest of my pint in one and walked towards the doors, I indulged in a burp and for a second I thought the greasy fish and chips were about to come back to haunt me.

Outside, half a dozen or so teenage feral trainee gangsters had gathered; as I pushed past one of them they looked at my faded green hands; they probably thought I belonged to some other tribe. 'Grumpy Green Hand Boaty's innit bro' respec.' I had another greasy belch and hobbled off back to the boat. It was raining again and the woman in the bedroom was still typing. This was possibly my shortest night out ever and even compared to the Traf, had to be one of the most disappointing.

Fortunately, I kept a few cans of beer on board for situations like this and I sat up quite late by my standards that night. Apart from enjoying my beer in peace, it gave the feral youths time to dissipate, so that I could relax properly at last. However, I was woken by one of the local boy racer imbeciles, I didn't dare look at what the time was, it was still dark and because it was mid-June, I estimated it to be before four a.m. The car roared right through the village going at some ridiculous speed in second gear, engine backfiring and the exhaust barking. I lay there listening for a good ten minutes, thinking that surely the speed this idiot was going at he must be on the outskirts of Burton on Trent by now. I felt a rush of anger and adrenaline and wondered how many households he had disturbed on his way ...ah bless 'em. I sat up, wide awake now and I remember having another little belch, I could still taste the greasy fish and chips, then looked at the inside of the roof for some time before I fell asleep again.

I got up around eight, the next morning, had my porridge and started the engine. It had rained all night and looking at the sky, it would not be long before it was raining again. Huge Cumuli Nimbus clouds bubbled up, already the height of the Himalayas but at least it was warmer today. I had only gone a few hundred yards when passed a lovely looking pub called the *Gate*; obviously the place the dog walker had recommended and it looked splendid; if only I had walked the other way last night! So, now, there were a few locks to get through of course, and then I was on my way to pastures new.

The rain came down in lumps big enough to injure mice and other small animals, then it stopped briefly while the sun attempted to come through. A short while later the sun gave up the ghost and it pissed down again. This continued for most of the morning. I came to a stretch where the tree branches came right down to the water, forming a canopy overhead. There were no other people to be seen, apart from the sound of the Lister engine chugging there was silence. Every time the rain stopped the trees would start to steam and I would not have been the least bit surprised if the Vietcong had sprung an ambush around the next bend. Slowly the day did become drier, but the sun made a complete retreat and the sky took on a uniform grey – again.

The canal was now bordered by wire fencing, punctuated every few hundred yards by red signs warning the public to Keep Out – this was an MOD training area. The sign said in effect, that if one ignored this warning and insisted on having a nosey round, then it would be a good idea not to touch anything that might be found innocently lying on the ground. Of course, some people just ignore all warnings and lose limbs – and more!

Every day of this journey I suffered some anxiety, knowing that at some point I would have to obtain supplies if I wanted to eat that evening and today was no different but because it was Sunday, I was more concerned than usual. (I have subsequently met a couple who live on a

111

delightful boat, which is kept in such pristine condition that cooking on board is forbidden. The owners are in the fortunate position to be able to eat out almost every day and should they stumble upon hard times, they buy an occasional supermarket ready-meal – Waitrose preferably. They are currently doing a grand tour of central Britain's waterways and restaurants, and why not?)

After twisting and turning, I arrived on the outskirts of Whittington in Staffordshire. Whittington is the Anglo Saxon for the farm or settlement of a person called Hwta or Hwittingas. However his name was pronounced, he certainly got around; my *Philip's Road Atlas* lists at least six other villages of the same name, stretching from Gloucestershire to Norfolk and then up to Lancashire.

About the only thing of interest en-route had been a loud noise and when I looked skywards, I saw a sight I had not seen in years. The last remaining Vulcan bomber had just taken off, presumably from an air show nearby and swooped overhead with its thunderous roar and black smoke pouring from the jet engines. In my childhood Vulcan's were quite a familiar sight, usually making their approaches back into RAF Finningley on the outskirts of Doncaster (This is now called Robin Hood Airport but no one quite knows why; if Robin did exist, he was never known to have frequented Doncaster, which is quite a way from Sherwood Forest). If the Vulcans were spotted side on and low on the horizon, they would appear to be wingless and were the cause of numerous UFO sightings throughout the sixties. My parents took to me to an open day at Finningley one year but the only things I remember are Bill Pertwee getting out of his Dr Who Tardis and the sight and sounds of a Vulcan taking off; the noise and vibration was incredible, it must have been hell for local residents.

It was now mid-afternoon and I needed to find a shop here in Whittington. My ancient hand-drawn map was always a challenge to read and though it was possible I had missed some other settlement (easy to overlook things, trying to scrutinise the map and steer at the same time), I could not see any other likely looking place. Of course, a lot of things like canal side superstores would not have existed when the author had sketched this chart with his best quill pen. I parked *Salamander* next to a likely looking road bridge where someone had kindly planted a sign pointing to the village and shop, even giving distances. As I bashed the mooring pins into the ground I saw there was some kind of social gathering going on at the house on the opposite bank. Most of the guests where sitting outside in the garden. Although the weather had not quite done a rewind back to early March, it certainly wasn't *Pimm's* weather. I briefly imagined myself going amongst the cold and semi-frozen guests amazing them with my sleight of hand and witty patter.

There was nothing particularly remarkable about this village, except that everyone I spoke to seemed very friendly and helpful and it doesn't take much to create a good feeling. In another hour, I was on my way again towards Fradley Junction. I was learning not to get too excited about what these grand-sounding junctions had to offer; usually it was a couple of locks, an awkward bridge, maybe a pub and often a sign pointing and giving the distance to some obscure milepost that would have had some significance 180 years ago – *Derwent Mouth 45Miles* or *Shadlow End 54 miles* – I made myself a pledge that I would go to both of these mystical places one day – or at least, I will have a look at them on a map.

Fradley Junction was a fairly straightforward arrangement by canal junction standards. Spanning the cut in front of me was a bridge with headroom of only nine inches but after a few seconds, I realised it either lifted or swung out of the way. I could see the scene was quite busy further on with lots of moored boats littered around and where I was looking seemed as good as anywhere so I got busy with the mooring up routine. Just to complete the late winter/early spring feel to the afternoon there was quite a wind blowing now. I got the first line secured but when I looked up half of the boat had drifted at 45% across the canal, giving me a strong deja-vu feeling of what felt like only a few days ago but was actually eight days previously at Soulbury. The boat was stuck on the bottom again, which I suppose was a better option than it floating at the mercy of the wind and the ever-shortening length of remaining mooring rope in my hands. An elderly looking couple now appeared, both dressed in what appeared to be 1950's style clothes and when they saw my predicament they kindly stopped to help. Between the three of us we managed to rock *Salamander* off the 'Goodwin Sands' and got her tamed along the towpath. The woman took the mooring pins off me and bashed them in to the ground. As I have said before, there are some amazing people afloat. Once the crisis was over we got into conversation. Although these two were not youngsters, they lived on their boat all year round and went all over the country, continuously cruising. They didn't say exactly where they came from but they had quite strong 'Black Country' accents and I had to really listen and then think for a few seconds, allowing the synapses to work before answering. Every time the woman spoke I thought of Mrs Overall from *Acorn Antiques*. I began to get a bit restless now; with darkness falling and with the onset of hypothermia, I was starting to wonder if they would ever stop talking. Eventually they said their farewells and wished me luck and I could finally dive inside the boat get the broken kettle on and the fire roaring.

Once I had got myself fed, watered, showered and warm, I thought I would do a bit of exploring but stepping outside, my suspicions were confirmed. *Salamander* was on the bottom again, as if stuck with aquatic epoxy resin but at least she was safe from speeding hire boats so I left her be. Once the initial sensations of being afloat subside, there is very little detectable movement inside a narrow boat so it is easy to completely forget one is afloat. (Although at times, during the storms of January and February in 2014, I was convinced I would wake the next day to see the Thames Barrier or Beachy Head outside the window, rather than Cassiobury Basin, Watford). Conversely, the brain quickly picks up the subtle messages when the boat is aground and there really is no movement. To this day, I sometimes find myself feeling the floor shift whilst shopping in Aldi, or the girl in the bank asking if I am all right, as I suddenly pause and stumble slightly for no apparent reason. As if I am the only person aware of the 2.3 magnitude earth tremor-taking place. This can't just be me; I must try and remember to mention it to other boaters; I always find showers on dry land tend to induce the sensation most.

Once I had walked past the line of moored boats, I could see directly facing the tee junction, was the slightly famous

Swan Inn which looked quite inviting, stuck in the middle of a terrace of buildings but just as I was contemplating going inside for a few pints, four bikers came out of the door and proceeded to go through the ritual of revving their engines for no apparent reason. When I start my car's engine, it just runs without any further intervention and even my ancient boat engine does the same. I had a motorbike myself for a couple of years, though I didn't ride it much after the time I slid off it on a patch of ice. The engine didn't need revving on that one either but these four just revved and revved, loudly, for ages, I abandoned any ideas of going into the pub now and even back on my boat a quarter mile away, I could still hear them revving.

As was often the case as fatigue increased, I can't remember a great deal about that evening and I awoke the next day to glorious June weather.

Chapter 10

Great – or Was It Little- Haywood

Within minutes I was at the peculiar swing bridge, the one that cleared the water by nine inches. I was just about to step off when a gentleman who had just come through the other way saw me and offered operate it for me. This was very kind of him and I felt the day had got off to a good start. Turning left at the junction I was now on the Trent and Mersey Canal, thinking this would just about chop the country into two halves. If they had built it further south it could have been the official border to a divided nation!

As I rounded the corner I could see there were several boats already waiting to go through the three locks only about one hundred yards further on, so anticipating a wait, I steered the boat in towards the canal side. I didn't need to slow down much, I had barely got going. A woman waved and shouted quite excitably that there were boats coming the other way; I nodded, saying I knew and was already about to stop. Because of the volume of traffic here with about five boats in each direction, it took almost three hours just to go the first mile but I didn't really mind because it was a beautiful summer day at last with birds singing and the bees were busy again too; I wondered where they all go to when the weather is miserable. The only thing that spoilt the peace was the occasional roar of one of our biker friends, making sure his machine could still do 0 to 160 in 10 seconds – in 2nd gear.

Eventually the bottleneck cleared and I was on my way proper. Considering this was not far from Burton-on-Trent, the scenery was quite pleasant. I'm not saying that Burton is not a nice place, just that I was surprised at the surroundings. I have often said that within a five-minute walk of wherever one goes in the British Isles, there is always pleasant scenery – except in Norfolk, where I have never seen anything to inspire me, although I was quite surprised to see some carrots growing in a field there once; when was the last time you saw anything other than rapeseed growing in a British field?

This was turning out to be the hottest day for some time and I was starting to feel quite uncomfortable, the heat from the engine didn't make things feel any easier. As I came around a sweeping bend, a huge factory appeared on my left. The walls were red brick and hugged the contours of the canal for hundreds of yards, I was going by it for a good ten minutes. I did not see a soul and wondered if the place was still in production. There was a bit of a quiet hum and that was all. From looking at the map, I knew this place was called Armitage. When I had mentioned the route I would be taking to Simon, he was quite enthusiastic, telling me about how well he knew this area and how he worked around here in his younger days and again later, with the army. This factory had me fascinated and I wanted to know what it was (The penny still hadn't dropped – there was a clue in the name of the place). Another boat going the opposite way came into view and I slowed my engine right down to tick-over; I wanted to be able hear the driver's response. After the usual pleasantries, I asked what the factory made.

'Toilets mate – you know – *Armitage Shanks*! Look, there are loads of them stock-piled outside.'

He was right too, there were thousands of them. Feeling a bit stupid, I said 'Oh yeah of course, thanks.' How could I have not guessed that? I had spent most of my life peeing into the damn things all over the world and how many times were they the last thing I saw before falling into drunken slumber? I thought about the name – was the company just called Shanks with the factory location added on out of politeness? Or was the company so vast they named the village after the company? Or maybe it was all a happy coincidence that a company named *Armitage Shanks* just happened to open a factory in a village called Armitage. (You can see how people go insane wondering about the universe and infinity whilst looking at the night sky.) Consulting *Google,* there is far more information given about *Armitage Shanks* toilet humour, water closet songs, film characters, poems etc. than about the company itself. Astonishingly this is not the only factory, they have seven more.

During all this deep thinking and wondering about WCs, two hire boats had snuck up behind and were now tailgating me and the scene was becoming increasingly urban as I approached Rugeley with other boats moored at every available gap all along the canal which meant that I could only proceed slowly but the crews of these two boats didn't seem to grasp the situation, or they weren't interested; they kept closing right up to me and then having to slow right down again to establish a gap. Just to add to the irritation they were having a constant loud conversation between the two boats shouting in Antipodean accents.

On one close encounter, I said; 'I can't go any faster, there are moored boats everywhere,' to which I got the inevitable reply:

'Yeah – cool – no worries.'

Just to make things even slower there were a couple of very tight bridges to go under, so that, apart from the lack of visibility, the hydraulic effect when the channel narrowed was bringing *Salamander* almost to a stop. I needed to go shopping of course, so when I spotted a convenient gap in what seemed to be the centre of Rugeley, I gratefully brought the boat to a halt, freeing the speed-seeking Aussies to roar all the way to their turnaround point, from which they could speed straight back to wherever they had come from.

The supermarket could not have been situated any more conveniently for canal creatures to go shopping, so for once, I could take my time wondering up and down the aisles but after a few minutes, I had an amnesia moment and couldn't remember where I was. I knew it was Tesco but didn't know which settlement; with planetary dim under way one Tesco is identical to the next throughout every town in Britain – and the world no doubt. I had a quick look around Rugeley and it all felt quite pleasant, although I didn't wander very far. It was a shame they had to build the huge coal fired power station so close to the town, I thought. Still not to worry, once we are totally dependent on China or Russia for all our energy needs, it won't be there much longer.

I had read somewhere that the river Trent followed the canal closely along this stretch but it was not mentioned on my ancient pirate map so I have no idea where I got the information but sure enough, I was getting frequent glimpses of the river, a fair distance below the canal level. Before I emigrated south, we would often venture into Lincolnshire on our cycling club runs, crossing the Trent at Gunness Wharf near Scunthorpe. I would always sneak a glance off to my left as we clattered over the swing bridge to see which vessels were moored close by. When I say vessels, these were proper ships and I was always amazed that something so large could navigate so far inland. There were usually a couple of coasters waiting to be filled or emptied; always registered to somewhere ridiculously exotic, such as Panama City, Montego Bay – or Goole.

This stretch of the Trent sparkled and rippled in the sunshine; the river was still quite juvenile here and its source was not far away up on the Staffordshire Moors. (I had a little fantasy about catching a lively trout from its waters.) In the distance to my left, I could see the uplands of Cannock Chase looming ever closer – the reason for my circuitous route – if this natural barrier did not exist, they could have sent the canal in a westerly direction instead of the north/south dog's leg route which would have made the journey a day or so shorter. Like my friends on the boats further south had advised me, this was a longer route but a lot easier

The lock at Colwich interrupted my progress; there was already another boat going in the same direction, also with a crew of one and I offered to help him through but he said he needed to call is wife to let her know where he was, so he waited and let me overtake, I couldn't help wondering why his wife was not on the boat with him. I chugged on for maybe another mile until I came to a pleasant looking spot on a gentle bend. A few boats were already moored here so I decided to join them – keeping a respectable distance of course.

It became apparent that I had stopped in the apex of a flattened "Y" shaped railway junction. On one side, the line veered off into the distance and on the other it ran almost parallel to the canal. Every fifteen minutes or so a Virgin Express train would stop almost opposite me and wait a few minutes for the signal to change, allowing it to proceed southward. This was obviously the West Coast Mainline again; I guessed the trains on the other line went to Stafford. I had completely forgotten this place had been the site of a serious train crash in 1986. The driver of one of the trains misunderstood the signal procedure and mistakenly thought he had a clear route across the junction. Two trains collided; the driver of one train was killed and 75 passengers were injured. Just writing this has jogged my memory and I do recall the accident but not that it happened so many years ago. In a different incident, a light aeroplane also managed to crash onto the junction in 2009 after getting in the way of some power cables. This time no trains were involved but the line was closed for several days after. If I had known or remembered all this I might have been inclined to stop a bit further upstream.

Despite the close proximity of the railway, I had a peaceful night and waking up to another beautiful day, I was soon on my way. It was surprisingly picturesque all along this stretch of canal, most of my way was tree-lined, providing shade from the glare of the sun and the river Trent continued to follow the canal tightly (More like the canal followed the river – the builders taking the obvious and easiest route). I looked for the Trent in my Philips Road Atlas the previous night but the detail was too vague, so I consulted *Google Earth* instead. I discovered it has a somewhat strange course, rising near Biddulph Moor just below the southern edge of the Peak District, then flowing south into Stoke (on Trent), adding several other brooks and tributaries on its way. It continues south to around Colwich but the direction then begins to alter, flowing east towards Burton on Trent. Eventually it takes an almost due northerly course becoming very large now, and finally plops into the Humber ninety something miles from its beginning, having done a complete 180% turn. I think that is quite remarkable and so was the 280lb, 8' 6" sturgeon that some startled angler once caught in it in 1902!

It was now just one mile to Great Haywood (though strangely, on the map Little Haywood appeared to be the larger of the two). The whole place looked interesting and complex from a boat point of view – I have no idea what the village itself was like, I never went there – first there was a lock to get through, guarded by an extremely low, tight bridge where it would have been easy to get off the boat, stumble up the steps to the top and if not paying attention, inflict a serious head injury. I wondered how many people had been brain damaged or decapitated over the years .Rumour had it that Ted, one of my Watford neighbours, had lost two (!) Asian wives due to low bridges. The first time, after searching the boat, it was only once he backtracked that he realised the awful truth.

Surviving this trap, I almost immediately came upon on a sharp left-hand turn. This was the junction with the

Staffordshire and Worcestershire Canal but it wasn't that obvious because the whole thing sat under a bridge, the purpose of which, apart from providing a path over the canal, was to block the sightline around the turn – and to hide the imminent approach of the single file aqueduct. If by now, you are shaking your head and muttering that I should have planned the passage better, remember I was still using a hand-drawn chart from circa 1800 which, as I have already mentioned, was rather vague. Besides I was knackered, and how many people attempt this sort of thing alone? In a more relaxed frame of mind, I have since looked at this in my later acquired *Collins and Nicholson Waterways Guide 4, Four Counties and the Welsh Canals*, which gives lots of information about Great Haywood, informing readers that there are some perfectly symmetrical cottages to be seen and there is a fresh fish shop behind the *Clifford Arms*. But unless I am mistaken, it does not mention that the aqueduct is only wide enough for one boat, and that this will not be apparent until it is too late to do anything about it!

I did manage to get across the aqueduct without meeting another boat which was very fortunate because I only just got onto it before four other boats were about to enter coming in the other direction. Once over the bridge, there were boats moored everywhere, narrowing the passage again. My luck ran out here and I had to stop get off and hold the boat by its lead, allowing a couple of boats to get by.

Once past the line of boats, I thought that I had taken the wrong route – I was suddenly on a body of water roughly the same size as Lake Erie! I had arrived at Tixall Wide which was a very strange sight after several weeks of narrow canals, and especially after the last ten minutes of extremely confined surroundings.!, The thought crossed my mind did the engineer of the canal James Brindley hold a competition? The winner would be the person who came up with the most imaginative and inspiring name for the new lake! There are two different stories about how the 'wide' came to be. When the canal was built in 1771 the owner and resident of Tixall Hall, Thomas Clifford agreed that the builders could traverse his land on the condition that from his favourite window view the canal would take on the appearance of a huge lake. The other explanation is that the lake already existed, so Clifford requested that the canal could incorporate it (because they were all nuts in those days), either version sounded plausible to me. When I was learning to fish in my early teens, I spent hours reading accounts by the father of all anglers, Izaak Walton who apparently learnt to catch fish on this very lake (A bit of a Robin Hood story that – if the second account of the lake isn't true, then the Walton story must be a lie too). Either way, the scene looked rather nice. the only part of the hall still remaining is the gatehouse, which is itself rather grand looking. There were about 500 boats moored here with most of the occupants already clutching cans of beer – and it was only ten thirty!

Chapter 11

Staffordshire and Worcestershire Canal

After Tixall lock, the canal twisted and turned around Milford and Baswich, avoiding the top north end of Cannock Chase, the map showing a course that looked something like the profile of the Eiger. I had come up the gentler side to the summit and would now be descending its steep north face. This exaggerated route was necessary to avoid going through the centre of Baswich, which looked to be dense with houses.

After this detour, the canal straightened for about three quarters of a mile and I was suddenly wrenched out of my usual bored daydream by the sight of what looked something like the Severn Bore approaching. It was still some way away and I struggled to focus properly, slowing the boat down to tick-over speed. I may be prone to exaggerate slightly but trust me on this occasion, this definitely looked like a small Tsunami coming towards me; there was a boat coming towards me so fast that its wake was coming over the edge of the canal and completely engulfing the towpath. I stood there with my mouth open, watching this spectacle hurtle towards me. *Salamander* started to rock from side to side and by the time Donald Campbell's ghost got level with me, I was well and truly aground. I was more astonished to see it looked like it was privately owned and not a hire vessel and the driver made no adjustment to his speed as he went by. This all happened too fast for me to be annoyed but I muttered something about being pushed aground.

The racer was around forty, sun-tanned and quite fat and I immediately judged him to be easily provoked into violence. Finally, I think the penny dropped and fat boy caught on that I was not too pleased and his behaviour was not what was expected. Speeding past me, he said in the broadest Wolverhampton accent;

'Oh they wunt to get this canal drudged.'

I couldn't think of anything suitably witty or sarcastic on the spur of the moment and just shouted; 'Yes and you need to bloody slow down!' (I probably used stronger language.)

I got the expected reply: 'What's up, have yow got a problem?'

I repeated what I had just said – this time without the swearing. And that was it – he was gone and I was left stuck to the bottom – again. It took a fair bit of heaving and straining with the barge pole to free *Salamander* from her sticky muddy prison and I was left angry and muttering to myself. Arsehole!

Underway again, I saw a young couple having a bit of a grope on the opposite bank which seemed like a funny place for a public show of affection until I remembered how, in a previous life I had done the same thing on a railway station in St Albans. It all seemed really exiting with trains zooming past at over one hundred miles per hour. The woman and I chuckled (Yes, there were two of us) and I said to her that the trains were going so fast at that point that people would not be able to see anything properly but they would just get a subliminal memory recall later, not knowing if they had really seen something going on or if they had just perhaps imagined it. Rather like in cinemas years ago when they allegedly and it transpired illegally, superimposed pictures of food items every four frames during the film to make people inexplicably crave a giant bag of popcorn or ten *Westlers* beef burgers . When I got level with the couple they sat up, looking a bit guilty, confirming they had indeed been up to some hanky-panky. I smiled at them commenting that I was surprised they had not both been swept into the canal by the recent 'parting of the waves'. They had no idea what I was talking about and I further diluted the impact by explaining about the previous boat going by too fast. The only thing worse than having to explain a joke, is explaining a magic trick – not how it is done, that is secret – but the effect. I know this because I am sometimes guilty of it. The youngsters laughed nervously, as people do when someone is gibbering rubbish but they feel obliged to humour them.

I was now going past the smartest, poshest marina I had seen so far, not that I had viewed many but this one looked something like you would expect with its clubhouse and blue ensign taking pride of place. I wondered if the recently encountered Staffordshire and Worcestershire Canal hydrofoil thug was a member of the Stafford Boat Club. Before much longer I came to the first of five locks indicating I was now getting close to Penkridge. Near the third lock at Longford, I noticed a car stop on the bridge and the occupant get out. I had an uneasy feeling about why

the vehicle had stopped at the dead centre of the bridge and
to add a bit more suspense, the driver was now looking over
the parapet, anticipating the boat reappearing through the
arch. I could sense by his body language that this reception
was all for me and tried to come up with a plan in case I
was confronted with a paving slab or half a dozen bricks.
I had no ideas and felt quite helpless and vulnerable. The
man continued to watch me as I emerged from under the
bridge. I could see he had quite an array of tattoos, most
of which looked like he had done them himself (possibly
with a *Sharpie* permanent marker pen). As if that was not
enough, he looked fairly handy too; no doubt a bit of a
scrapper. Putting my best magician's cold-reading skills to
work, I guessed he might have been ex-Infantry, a bouncer,
a lag – or maybe all of those. Either way, he looked a lot
younger, fitter and harder than me – if this one started I
would have a problem.

I stopped to get ready to do the lock thing for about the
hundredth time, at the same time watching my new friend
approach. He asked me if I was all right, to which I replied
that I was. He then asked where I was going and I told him.
Lighting a cigarette, he asked me if I wanted one. I don't
smoke but not wanting to offend, I took one and began to
relax a bit, feeling quite light-headed from the nicotine. We
had a bit of a chat and he actually seemed all right. I told
him about the speeding moron a few miles back. Tattoo
man further confirmed my suspicion by stating there would
have been justifiable violence had it been himself involved;
my unease returned. I was about to open the lock paddles
when he said to give him the windlass; he would do the
hard work and I could stay on the boat. I had a little mental

conversation; he will either attack me with the windlass or jump into his car with it and drive off, leaving me helpless and stranded with no way of operating the lock! None of these things happened – just has he was about to wind the last ratchet, his phone rang.

After a few seconds, he said; ' I've got to go'.

And he did; leaving the windlass hanging onto the mechanism. I thought – how bizarre – and went on my way as if nothing had ever happened – much relieved nonetheless.

Penkeridge was all a-bustle with boats and boat people. I was just about to fasten my boat to the only apparent free space between here and Ellesmere Port, when a man came walking by with his family. His teenage daughter gave me a lovely smile, looking at me for a split second longer than politeness called for, so I gave her a smile back. (There are some young women who like older men you know – just ask Michael Douglas junior – if he is still alive – anyway I am often told I look younger than my age) Her father caught us in our little flirt but didn't seem too concerned, just saying to me; 'You can't moor there, it's a winding hole.' I was familiar with this term (for the non-boaters, this is a largish area reserved for turning a boat around in; etiquette and rules prohibit any mooring next to a winding hole.) Because of words like 'winding', 'bear' and 'row' it always amazes me that foreigners ever learn to speak English at all, let alone so well. Until now, I had only ever seen the word written in reference to canals and assumed it was pronounced *wine-ding,* like cotton on a reel, or turning a handle on a DAB radio. This chap though, pronounced the word *winding*, like turbulent weather or flatulence. This mispronunciation, in a Black Country accent, made me smile even more . To make things worse, he repeated the whole thing again but it turns out he would have had the last laugh had I been arrogant enough to try and correct him because I later discovered his pronunciation was probably correct and the term originates from the old days when the prevailing wind would have been used to turn boats around – although like most things boat related – there is lots of debate on the subject.

Taking the man's advice, I moved a bit further along and found a more suitable place to lie up for the night. Due to accumulated fatigue and bone idleness, the inside of the boat was beginning to look something like downtown Rakka. My friend Simon had arranged to travel from Oswestry to join me for the day tomorrow. This would be the first time he had seen my boat and I wanted to create a good impression. Having virtually no food on board meant I would have to go shopping again if I wanted to eat. I was already tired but I would have to walk – shop – walk – cook – and then clean. Simon had said that Penkeridge was an attractive little town or large village and so it was; full of character with half-timbered buildings everywhere. Most importantly, they had a proper supermarket where the prices were just about affordable. After buying my usual pasta, Dolmio sauce, a head of broccoli, a bottle of milk and bread I had a little wander around. Ten minutes later, I had seen just about all that Penkeridge had to offer and began to make my way back to the boat. There was a pub next to the canal and stepping off the road, I cut through the back yard. It was six-ish and the place was full of families enjoying an early evening drink or a meal when a motorbike manifested itself right in the middle and began an engine-revving demonstration. Within seconds every child within earshot was crying and all the dogs in a half- mile radius joined in trying to out-bark each other. The other guests, who weren't crying or barking, just looked at each other, bewildered. After a few minutes, the rider of the machine looked around confused, as if he too, did not understand what was happening. Finally, he shunted his bike round to face the exit and roared off. The noise eventually faded into the distance and the head-shaking customers resumed their evening.

I made myself yet another brew, drank it and got stuck into boat cleaning. An hour later I sat down to another brew, feeling relaxed and vowing to keep things looking the way they were now. In reality, all I had to do was make a sandwich and the galley would look untidy again. Most of my food preparation was done with a chopping board balanced at 45% on the edge of the sink. I am not sure when the first domestic gas cooker was introduced but my white and red *Flavel Courier* must be one of the earliest ever built. I attempted to slide it out from the position it had held since 1978, intending to give the sides of the cooker a damned good clean. I managed to heave it about six inches forward when jammed and stubbornly refused to move again – in any direction. So now it is stuck forward of where it belongs, giving a tantalising glimpse of decades of accumulated grease and grime. Oh – and the top isn't level any more, consequently all liquids appear to boil at a 15% angle. Strangely, the oven is without a shadow of doubt, the best and most accurate I have ever used -anywhere. Shame about the Salamander/grill though.

I fiddled with the TV aerial as I did every evening. Standing on the roof I pointed it away from where I estimated the largest population would be, in this case, Wolverhampton. I then scurried inside and waited (ten minutes) for the auto-tune to complete and inform me it had found – zero programmes – not even Al Jazeera! I repeated the process, this time pointing the antennae towards where I thought Cannock Chase was – logic dictating this was the highest point for miles and therefore likely to be where the transmitter was. This went on for another hour while I tried the Pennines, the Black Mountains in Wales – and any other upland region within 150 miles I could remember the approximate direction of. Eventually I gave up and settled for crackling, hissing Radio 2 on the wind-up DAB radio. In fact, if I relied on the clockwork battery I could get decent reception, though it needed furious cranking every few minutes. Instead, I used the mains lead which made the radio sound a bit like a Morse code receiver. I would catch the odd spoken word here and there – just enough to get the gist of what was going on in the almost-forgotten outside world. From what I could gather, the breaking news was that Chris Evans was about to be appointed as next presenter of *Top Gear*. So, it was possible to find someone more irritating than Clarkson after all. There again, as George Osborne reminded us, we are all in it together!

I mentioned earlier that I had received some favourable comments from various people about the feat I was attempting. Like most daft things I have done over the years, I did not regard this journey as anything special but one evening on *Facebook*, someone suggested that this journey had not been done single-handed before. I took this as a complement (and with a shovel-full of salt) but it did make me think about things. Simon was coming to lend me a hand over several days so I could not claim in truth to have done the whole thing alone. I was not stubborn or stupid enough to refuse his help though. Indeed, the very next day, there would be several stretches of this canal that although not impossible, would be foolish or even dangerous to cruise alone. I was up and about early next day; there were still a few last-minute cleaning jobs to be done before my visitor arrived. I didn't know exactly what time Simon would turn up; he still had to find and identify *Salamander* and I don't like surprises.

Whilst I busied myself, I listened to Radio 2 and the Chris Evans show, tolerating it for around twenty minutes before silencing it again. The whole subject of his monologue punctuating the odd bits of music here and there, was an excited babble about how wonderful it was that his BBC mates had agreed to let him present the new *Top Gear* show once the dust had settled on the previous controversial series. I have no idea which group Clarkson alienated or why. Other than getting from A to B in a realistic time, I have never had the slightest interest in cars. Eighteen months later, after all the excitement, this apparently was a complete one-episode disaster. What a shame.

True to his word, Simon knocked on the side of the boat at about nine. He was eager to steer and I was happy to let him so it was not too long before we arrived at the first of the six locks of the day. Finally, with a crew of two, I could grudgingly begin to see how this boating lark could be pleasurable; I operated all the locks while Simon did the driving. There was nothing remarkable about the scenery here and the uniform grey sky made everything look dull and dismal. Soon we were chugging past a huge chemical factory and just like all dodgy factories, there were no workers to be seen and no indication of what was being produced. Like *Armitage Shanks,* this place seemed to go on for miles (well about 3/4 of one). All we could see were lots of complicated pipe work and storage tanks. Every few hundred yards, a bundle of pipes leaped over the perimeter fence and the canal, forming a sort of bridge with one of those spiky wheels around it to deter local drunks and escaping mad scientists from doing death-defying walks along it. I wondered where the pipes went; the place had a horrible smell. More sinister though, were the many signs telling us that, should an alarm sound, we must put the boat into full steam ahead and get as far away from the place as possible. Another sign said Do Not Even Think of Mooring Here! Does the *Daily Mail* know about this place? I wondered. Simon and I watched it go by almost in silence, occasionally speculating to each other what it was they were brewing up. At least there were no houses built nearby.

The canal was starting to look like an aquatic version of the Cresta Run, twisting first one way then another. By now I had accepted that canal designers for some perverse reason, insisted on plonking bridges on nearly every blind bend they encountered but now the clearances under these were becoming ridiculously tight, threatening to decapitate the exhaust pipe if the boat was not kept exactly dead centre as we passed underneath. As each bridge came into sight I would carefully make my way along the gunwales down the sides of the boat and position myself at the front, remembering to keep my head out of the way of the ever-diminishing space available. The reason for my space walks (apart from the sheer thrill) was to get a good look at what might be coming towards us – the last thing we needed was a boat full of inebriated call centre staff from Milton Keynes coming the other way at fifteen knots. Eventually things widened out again, only for us to meet some very nervous looking youngsters who were learning to canoe; Simon anticipated what could happen and slowed to a crawl. With Weil's disease on most waterways in the country, I wonder how safe it can be to paddle a canoe on a canal; no matter how competent a paddler you are, at some point I thought, ingesting a huge mouthful of water is part and parcel of the pursuit.

Now the bank was becoming populated by depressed looking anglers spaced out at regular intervals; evidently a fishing match. To the uninitiated, the very notion of competitive fishing sounds baffling. Angling, darts and snooker are possibly the only sports where chain smoking and obesity are seen as an advantage. I will try to explain how it works; each competitor draws a peg (a designated stretch of water) at random and if you happen to get one without any fish in it, tough luck. A signal is given and everyone fishes for a pre-arranged length of time; the person who weighs in the heaviest keep-net at the end is the winner.

I first heard of this sport when I was about fourteen; things may have changed since but back then, there were two methods of catching a healthy bag of fish. The skilled or confident angler could target just a few large specimens to make up the weight – matches are often won with a total of only a couple of pounds and if conditions are not very productive – just one eight-foot sturgeon could usually win comfortably! The more usual method, is to try to catch a couple of hundred minnows, with each one weighing around half a gram. These would need to be caught at a rate of around one every twenty seconds for a period of four hours to secure a decent total weight. Tactics and equipment have changed over the years, hundreds of years ago our friendly fishing guru Izaac Walton, would have used a roach pole to catch his objects of desire. I remember reading about these in a fantastic book containing lots of fishing adventure stories by different authors, Walton included. Roach poles were primitive fishing rods. The fishing reel hadn't yet been invented and neither had Fluorocarbon line. They were dozens of feet long with a fixed length of line, probably braided horsehair or catgut, attached to the business end. The pole, bait and hook were simply dangled where the fish were expected to be and when one was hooked, the pole would be broken down section by section until the end of the line could be grabbed.

Over the years, centre pin reels and later still, fixed spool reels made life a lot easier and when I rode along canal towpaths twenty-odd years ago, I was surprised to see that the discerning angler in the latter part of the 20th century, were almost exclusively using poles (albeit now made from carbon fibre and costing just slightly less than a light aeroplane). In subsequent conversations with the odd sociable angler, I would express my astonishment that something from the 16th century was so popular again but no one could give me a convincing reason why they are better than a rod and reel. Maybe one day, horses and carts will be commonplace again on the M6 turnpike road, along with clay vapour pipes! One of the anglers stood out from the rest because he smiled. I asked if he had had any luck to which he replied;

'Nowt.'

I made the same enquiry further along and got the same answer; it certainly wasn't the intense sunshine or the heat that was spoiling the fishes' appetite.

Whether it was intentional or coincidental that Simon had chosen to join me today, his help could not have been timelier. We were now approaching a very narrow cutting and I assumed my position complete with red flag as lookout at the front of *Salamander*, peering into the distance. The channel was totally blind with no passing places which would have been interesting to say the least, if I had been alone but we survived the rock alley and found ourselves on the outskirts of Wolverhampton. The canal wandered through a meadow with lots of green reeds lining the banks and across the field was an estate of rather nice-looking detached houses but I wasn't entirely sure if I wanted to spend the night here. A man walking his dog came over for a chat and was astonished to hear I had sailed the boat all the way from Watford single-handed. When Watford is mentioned in conversation, the Hertfordshire town is often confused with Watford Gap, around forty-five miles to the north, in Northamptonshire. Ernie, an incredibly friendly coach driver from back home spotted me one evening in the local drinking den just after I had moved south again. He said he had not seen me for a while and I mentioned Watford. 'Oh yeah, I know Watford, I always stop off at the services when I am driving the bus to France – hmm yeah – Watford Gap, know it well.' I remember turning to my mate Steve saying; 'Just think, if Ernie was an airline pilot, he could take off for Paris in France and land nine hours later in Texas.' Anyway, the chap on the canal really did know where Watford was because he often went on company courses there. He assured me it was safe to camp here overnight so I got busy with the hammer and mooring pins; wherever I tried to bash one in, there were reeds in the way but after about fifteen minutes, I was satisfied the boat would not wander off while I slept. Simon was now facing around a ten-mile bike ride back to Penkeridge where his van was parked and he arranged to meet me again the day after next, having some other business planned for the following day. After thanking him, I watched him pedal off along the towpath just as the rain started to pour. Feeling slightly guilty, I went inside again to get the fire going.

The dog walker had told me there was a Morrison's supermarket just around the corner, so after a brew and a shower I set off to find it. Sure enough, there it was a couple of hundred yards away. I had to walk through a precinct where two teenagers, a boy and a girl were sitting on a bench. Judging by the amount of smoke they were producing, I thought they had lit up a spliff but when I got closer, it looked more like a crack pipe they were sharing. I was quite shocked and realised what a sheltered life I had led so far. When I came back ten minutes later, they were both zooming around the precinct on skateboards. I had a good look; they could not have been more than fourteen.

By the time I got back to *Salamander* I had a new neighbour; an angler had made himself a hide in the middle of the reeds right next to the boat. I gave him a greeting and he seemed quite friendly so we talked for a few minutes, exchanging exaggerated tales of fish we had caught over the years, both using outstretched hands in the time-honoured manner to illustrate the size of the fish involved. Eventually I said I was going inside where it was warm and the fisherman said he would stay where he was until it got dark, or something more exciting happened. Because of the close proximity of the urban surroundings, I was tempted to connect the generator to the mooring pins that night!

Chapter 12

The Shroppie

I was quite relieved next day to find I had neither been burgled nor had the boat set alight during the night; the area did not look too bad but the proximity to Wolverhampton had made me feel uneasy, there had been some incidents here involving canals and boats. The most recent one involved draining all the locks for miles when no one was looking. No one seemed to know how it was possible but I saw a photo, probably on Facebook, of a canal which was now just a wide shopping-trolley-filled trench.

I had only less than a mile to go now and I would be onto the Shropshire Union Canal or the 'Shroppie', as they say in the vernacular, with well over 2/3 of my journey cracked – I was beginning to see the light. Once again, the layout at Autherley Junction had been designed to catch out the not-so-alert boater; going under the Blaydon Road Bridge, I immediately came to the right turn that would take me onto the 'Shroppie'. This turn was very tight, almost doubling back on itself and no sooner was I round it there was the stop lock – why did they design these locations to be so difficult? I was now travelling north west again, after yet another near-360% turn, passing behind the houses and other buildings where I had seen the crack-smoking skate boarders the night before. Immediately after the stop lock there was an appealing looking boat yard and chandler's shop and I remembered it would probably be a good idea to think about taking some more fuel on board. The chap in the shop told me their diesel was quite expensive and if I could hang on, there was a place further up the cut where the 'fuel was so cheap they almost gave it away'. I got the distinct impression this was not the owner I was speaking to. I thanked the assistant for his help and honesty, bought myself a *Magnum* ice cream for my second breakfast and received about £1.20 change from my fiver, then got on my way. The scenery was becoming rural once more and the sun was shining, although it still felt more like mid-April than midsummer.

I was on the approach to Brewood, which Simon had already told me, is pronounced Brood, to save me from further embarrassment should the colloquial pronunciation police be listening. It was getting quite busy around here; I went through several bridges and gave way to other boats coming towards me but none of them bothered to thank me. I said good morning to a couple on another boat as they went by and was just ignored, so I decided not to waste any more breath unless I was spoken to first; Brewood, attractive as it was, must be the Henley on Thames of the Midlands and I had no intention of stopping there. Hard to believe I was only a few miles from Wolverhampton – I felt sure most people would say hello there.

Soon after leaving Brewood, I trundled over Stretton Aqueduct. There was nothing very exciting about the aqueduct itself, it was really just a short bridge spanning a road but the canal here was at quite a substantial height above the A5 trunk road and it created quite a surreal scenario. There was a brief glimpse of speeding vehicles roaring by dozens of feet below and then, just as suddenly, everything was tranquil once more...except for the Lister engine. It must have been even stranger from the viewpoint of the motorists below if they were strangers to the area. The appearance of a narrow boat crossing the road would probably be the last thing they expected to see. Once during an exercise in northern Germany, almost on the Danish border, the conversation in our Land Rover was abruptly ended when we simultaneously noticed a huge ocean-going ship, apparently plodding along through the very flat fields and past the beige cows of Schleswig-Holstein. After a moment, we remembered that the Kiel Ship Canal came this way, shortening the route from the North Sea to the Baltic by a considerable distance. We then continued our discussion on the merits of German women in comparison to our own – where we could procure our next Bratwurst from – and would the 'Compo' field-ration curry still be safe to eat after adding a few more bits and pieces and re-heating it for the fifth time.

I had just gone under a bridge when I saw a short jetty with what looked like a petrol pump – this must be the place where the cheap fuel could be obtained. Putting *Salamander* into reverse gear, I just managed to get her moored to the jetty, having almost overrun it. A set of steep wooden steps led up to the road level and right next to the bridge was the garage/cum/chandlers. Outside was a pair of vintage petrol pumps with analogue dials, looking like comical space aliens with their huge white bulbous heads adorned with the word 'Shell'. It's only at times like this we realise how quickly things alter without us noticing

Stepping inside, the place looked like a 1950s working museum, with little packets of bits and bobs that I hadn't seen in years, lying about everywhere. I thought perhaps I had got the wrong place but a few words with the attendant confirmed that I could indeed buy as much red diesel as I liked, for an unbelievable price of 57p per litre. Just a year before, I had been forking out £1.20 per litre. I filled *Salamander* until I got bored and the tank looked healthily full; again it was on a do-it-yourself basis. Back up the steps on dry land, I settled my bill. Talking to the garage attendant or proprietor, I commented that the system of paying different taxes depending on what the fuel was used for, seemed particularly nonsensical when you made your own declaration of what percentage would be for travelling, heating, or filling the car! I asked if anyone ever checked these declarations as he wrote down the lies I had just told him into a ledger. He spent the next fifteen minutes or so explaining that since 1976, no-one had ever checked his paper work and he blamed the whole farcical system on the EU – well there's a surprise! With this re-supply, I would have more than enough fuel to get me to my final destination – and maybe see me through the following year as well.

Soon after this, I came to the only other lock of the day. There were no other customers around so I tied the boat to a steel bollard and taking a few minutes to take stock of my surroundings, I caught sight of something quite astonishing. I remember thinking I ought to take a photograph of this because no one will ever believe me and I have regretted not doing so ever since. People give me doubtful looks when I tell them that at Wheaton Aston lock, I saw the biggest goose ever – I am no expert on how big these things grow but this one was absolutely massive. It was at least four feet tall with feet only slightly smaller than my size nines. Not fancying another encounter with a man-eater after the ginger dogs of Marsworth locks incident, I decided I would not bother going around to its side of the lock but just take a bit longer to get through and only operate the paddles on my side. This gave me time to sit on the nearby bench and observe the thing at my leisure. The goose's drinking technique fascinated me; it would bend its neck until it could manoeuvre its beak horizontally level with the puddle and thrust its neck forward to fill the beak with water. It would then very slowly straighten up and finally tilt its beak backwards, allowing the water to flow down the length of its three-foot neck. This was repeated over and over until the goose was satisfied – no wonder they aren't allowed to go in pubs! This might be standard procedure for drinking geese but I couldn't help thinking that this strange carry-on was necessary because of the animal's size.

While I was watching all this, I sensed I was being watched myself and looking round, I saw a slightly familiar figure coming towards me. Suddenly I remembered the tattooed bridge watcher from a few days ago but now he was with a woman and they both wore *Canal and River Trust* T-shirts. It all made sense now: the pair of them worked, with or without pay, for what was now a charity, after the government had disowned the national canal network (along with many other things which don't make enough money for their cronies). He asked about my day's adventures so far and I mentioned the stuck-up people in Brewood, just stopping myself from pronouncing the place

Breewood, like I knew I would eventually. I said I intended to stop at Gnosall that night and struggled with that name too, almost pronouncing the 'G'.

'Tattoo' interjected: 'It's 'No-sorl.'

At the same time commenting that it was quite a decent place for an overnight stop. I said that I was surprised to bump into him again as it had been several days and lots of miles since our first meeting. I was brought back to reality when he laughed and said:

'It's about three miles from here to Penkeridge.'

Of course, with the south and north bound dog-leg route I had taken and travelling at an average speed of half a mile an hour, that would be correct. 'Tattoo man' helped me through the lock (without abandoning me this time) and mega-goose eyed me, in between scooping more water from muddy puddles on the other bank. I mentioned the bird to a passing local who just said; 'Oh that's George, he's been there for years,' as if a goose the size of an ostrich was perfectly normal.

I saw no more animal mutations that day and after a few miles, I arrived at Gnosall. The canal over-bridges here had gone from something like rabbit holes to the other extreme and now resembled the whispering gallery at St. Paul's Cathedral. Just like the ones at Fenny Stratford, the navvies who built this canal must have been conserving their bricks and stone. Suddenly realising they only had a few more miles to construct and decided to build the remainder of the structure with massive headroom, once again to avoid having tons of spare materials on their hands. The village looked quite attractive, with stone buildings hugging the canal but there were boats everywhere and I had to go beyond the village before I found somewhere to moor up. Spotting a gap in the line of boats just before an over-bridge, the spot looked ideal with the late afternoon sun filtering through the trees and bathing everything in yellow light.

I had noticed earlier that I had no phone signal and since the canal here was contained in a cutting, it was not very surprising that this place was no better. Simon had promised to come and help me again the next day so it was essential that I contact him, to let him know my location. So, gathering a few essentials together, I set off walking.

There were some steps leading up from the water to the top of the bank and a young chap was sitting with his children. He conveniently finished his own phone conversation as I approached and told him my predicament. He said reception was particularly bad in this area but if I walked through the village to the hill near the fish and chip shop, I would probably get a signal there. Since his phone seemed to be working perfectly, I had secretly hoped he would offer me the use of it but he either did not take the hint or just did not want me to use it. I asked him how far it was and he told me it was about half a mile.

Setting off in the recommended direction, I walked and walked. Looking back, I cannot remember why I had such a sense of urgency, unless it was that I did not want to spend the entire evening traipsing around rural Staffordshire until darkness fell. Amongst other physical tortures, the army have something known as 'tabbing' (they also love abbreviations and acronyms). 'Tabbing' means tactical advance to battle; this involves covering long distances on foot in the form of very fast marching, alternating with running. Regardless of fitness levels, everyone agreed that while they were doing the running phase, they would begin to fantasise about being shouted at to switch back to marching – but within seconds of reverting to quick marching – they would all long to start running again. This would go on for hours at a time and whether walking, running or bursting into flame, the speed and effort were the same. With your face almost resting on the backpack of the bloke in front of you – it was purgatory. The other thing peculiar to tabbing was that it induced agonising shin splints within the first few minutes of starting off – if you are not familiar with the term, shin splints make your lower legs feel like the bones are about to snap. If you have the tenacity to ignore the pain long enough, they can lead to stress fractures in the bone – and you do not want that when on holiday. This was happening to me now; things were not so urgent that I needed to run, so I stuck to just walking very fast, pausing now and then to flick the sweat off the end of my nose and check to see if the *'Three'* phone network had woken up yet – it hadn't.

I was about to give up when I saw the fish shop tucked away across the road and despite my near-death experience with the bag of grease in Amington, I decided to kill two birds with one stone and risk wasting another five pounds. It must be a weekly tradition in Gnosall that every resident buys fish and chips on a Thursday evening; the place was packed. My hands were more or less back to their normal colour now but the occupants of the shop still looked at me suspiciously – and dripping with sweat didn't improve the situation. A few years ago, whilst relieving myself in a pub toilet, the occupant of the next-door urinal glanced at me as he turned to walk away but suddenly stopped and with a beaming smile said:

'******* 'ell mate – it's you, isn't it?'

Standing there with not a clue what this lunatic was talking about, I confirmed that it was, indeed, me. He continued:

'**** me it's got to be you, you're 'im off the telly, aren't you?'

My mind was racing now, there were thousands of people on the telly, and I was just hoped he wasn't confusing me with George Osborne – or Susan Boyle.

'Sorry mate' I said; 'I haven't got a clue who you think I am.'

'You're that geezer on that program, that goes around fixing houses.' He insisted.

From that day to this, I have no idea who he had mistaken me for. The point is, that for some time now, judging by the number of strange looks I get almost everywhere I go, maybe people are confusing me with someone well known. Who knows, maybe George Clooney owns a narrowboat!

Shuffling along the queue I was eventually met with a scouring glare from one of the assistants.

'Yes?' she snarled.

Attempting a smile, I said; 'Er – cod chips and peas please,'

Glaring at me she said: 'What?'

I repeated it all again as the queue fell silent.

The little darling glared at me again and said, slightly more courteously; 'Pardon?'

Vaulting over the counter I dragged her over to the deep fryer, stabbing at a huge piece of cod with my finger and shouting; 'Look! Cod! That's what I would like – some of that fish – with some chips – you cretin!' *I didn't really do that, but it was tempting.*

After repeating my request for the third time, I got my message across, though it might have been easier to order a deep-fried swan in Polish, than it was to obtain cod and chips in Staffordshire.

'Salt and vinegar?' the girl asked.

'Oh yes please, and just a touch of arsenic.' I said, glaring back at her. In the end, the meal wasn't too bad and I gobbled it down, checking my dead phone and walking at a ridiculous pace at the same time.

Eventually I arrived back at the steps leading to the canal and my *Vodaphone* acquaintance was still there. He asked me how I had got along and resisting the temptation to comment on his woeful inability to estimate half a mile, I said that despite walking around four miles, I still could not get a phone signal. There was still no offer of using his phone, so wiping the sweat from my eyes, I staggered the last few hundred yards back to *Salamander* – checked my phone once more and there it was – a perfect five bar signal – unbelievable. Not trusting the transient signal, I called Simon immediately, not even pausing to put the kettle on to boil. He already knew Gnosall vaguely and because all the bridges on the canal system are numbered, it was easy for him to identify exactly where I and the boat were spending the night.

Some night it was too. Years ago, when I was married, I began to suffer with really terrifying dreams. I cannot really blame the ex-Mrs Farmer because the night terrors continued even after she had long gone to wherever it was. This nonsense went on for a number of years and only slowly diminished but occasionally, to this day, I still have bizarre dreams that seem utterly real. The really scary bit is that when I eventually wake from my terror, whatever I have just experienced asleep, continues in a waking state – often for several minutes.

Let me just get comfortable on the couch and I will tell you about some of the crazy stuff I have suffered in my dreams over the years. I have had all my teeth pulled out by nasty people, almost drowned quite a few times, swallowed handfuls of sewing needles and had my fingers cut off one by one, with a pair of blunt scissors – this particular night, I dreamt the boat was cruising down the canal on its own while I slept. It happened three times and each time, I leapt from my bed, trying to get onto the stern and take control of the boat. Luckily, I woke up fully just before I got outside and tried to run on water. With my heart pounding in my chest like some crazed cartoon character, I slowly realised each time, that it was a dream.

I looked around coyly in case someone had seen my deranged nocturnal anguish. I once tried to read a book by the famous shrink Carl Jung, titled *Man and His Symbols* which was all about dreams and their meanings – maybe I should attempt to read it again! The last bout of madness a few months ago, involved being attacked by huge silent dogs which bit my neck, vampire style, this happened for a couple of nights over a few weeks. On a more benign note, I now have frequent dreams about stalking huge, transparent trout in a fast-flowing river!

After this traumatic night, a wood pigeon woke me at around 03.45, sounding as if it was in the tree right above the boat. I suppose you have to admire their determination but once started, the damn thing coo-cooed for hours. I tossed and turned until around seven and got up feeling knackered – but relieved to find that *Salamander* was still in exactly the same place as I had left her.

I had assumed, again wrongly, that the bridge over the canal carried a road over the water that Simon would be able to drive over and would see the sparkling green boat below. I did a quick, 'recce' only to discover that it was not a metalled road but just a rough farm track. I needed to act quickly and head him off on the main road – the last thing I wanted was for him and his partner Linda, spending the day searching for me after quite a long drive from Oswestry. Setting off once more at combat fitness test speed, I headed for the bridge some way behind me, where the main road was. After last night's walk, my legs were feeling quite stiff and the dreaded shin splints started almost immediately. There was an obvious looking junction next to a pub just up the road from the bridge, I was not exactly sure which direction my friends would appear from, so I decided this would be the sensible place to wait. Ten minutes later a white van appeared, indicated left and drove straight past me; I recognised Linda and Simon inside. Watching the van disappear up the road in the same direction I had just come from, I started to run but after a few yards I realised the futility of trying to chase a van on foot. I walked further up the road thinking that I was about to waste an entire day chasing a van around the back lanes of Staffordshire. After a few more minutes, the van reappeared coming back towards me and this time, they saw me and stopped. I explained the situation to them and we ended up doing a bit of a detour on foot after parking the van. Then it turned out there was no access from the footpath bridge down to the canal, where the boat lay, tantalisingly close to us, so we ended up retracing our steps all the way back from where I had chased the van, this time though, our hands were full of the various bags of food and goodies Linda had kindly brought along – just in case we got stranded in a blizzard and could not get to a shop for a few days!

After a bit more fussing we got on our way. Linda asked me what I had to eat the previous night and I told her that it was a bit of a long story . Simon said I looked tired, so I told them both about my '*Hammer House of Horror*' dream saga and they both looked at me aghast. Simon was driving again, Linda vanished inside for ages and eventually re-appeared with a lovely bacon sandwich and a mug of tea for the two sailors. With no locks in sight for miles, I enjoyed my redundancy, stuffed myself with the sarnie and relaxed a bit. After the shaky start and the nocturnal demons, the day started to feel pleasant.

We plodded on, crossing the Shelmore Embankment which the *Collins Guide* managed as usual, to make sound much more interesting than it actually was. Apparently, it was a nightmare to build (could be material there for my future dreams), bursting its banks on occasion, leaving boats (and giant geese) floundering on the muddy bottom. During the war, it was considered risky, a possible target for German bombers with the potential to flood the outlying land. There are still floodgates at each end so it can be isolated in case it misbehaves again.

I had heard of Norbury Junction before but I may have confused it with the railway junction of the same name, which I believe is somewhere in London. Originally, the branch would have gone on to Newport (Salop) and further to Shrewsbury but if we had all blinked at once, we could easily have missed it, as all that remains, like so many other grand-sounding latter-day canal centres, was a short stub which went nowhere. It should really have been renamed just Norbury! Though to be fair, there were a number of boaty-type facilities there, we didn't need anything, so pressed on, chugging through the romantically named Grub Street cutting with its iconic tall double-decked bridge complete with its bizarre half telegraph pole set between its tiers – there are certainly some weird structures on our canals.

We stopped briefly for Linda to stock up the food supplies from one of the delightful stands that had begun to appear here and there, offering cakes, pork pies, sausage, bacon and what-have-you. It is quite reassuring to know that even in this age, people are still prepared to leave goods unattended and to rely on the honesty of customers to throw a few quid into the box after helping themselves to whatever is on offer. Looking around, Simon pointed out an old wooden factory building with a hoist still in place that would have been used to load and unload boats when they came alongside. I thought it would make a good companion for the 1950's garage the other day but this place was really old looking, with original enamel signs, advertising Fry's chocolate and other long forgotten items. I assumed it would have been closed down soon after WW1 but Simon said it was still in production! I had a look in the good old *Collins Guide* and indeed, it had been a chocolate factory once but now it made Birds Custard, Angel Delight and other products, full of E numbers and lecithin. There was no sound and it was hard to believe it was still operating – just like all the other factories viewed so far on this journey – not a human to be seen!

Suddenly we came up behind five or six hire boats, looking like a bunch of drunks trying to walk on ice. The canal here was ridiculously shallow and a couple of the boats had run aground while the other crews had panicked and tried to stop so that chaos ensued with boats going all over the place.

Another boat – a private one, appeared behind us blasting its horn and pushing through the carnage. The skipper looked like a stand-in for the country singer Willy Nelson – complete with long grey ponytail and beard! I had always considered Simon to be a bit more restrained than me but I could see a bit of red mist appearing. As soon as 'Willy' went by, Simon grinned and put *Salamander* into full steam ahead, saying he was just going to give 'Mr. Impatient' a bit of a nudge, just to let him know that it was not exclusively his canal. So, we rammed him – gently – as Simon said – nothing too violent. 'Willy' looked quite startled but said nothing. I think he got the message, I was tempted to start singing; "*To all the girls I've loved before*". He didn't slow down however, and was soon out of sight, which was perhaps just as well. Being politer, we waited for the other boats to regain their composure before pushing on towards Market Drayton and ever closer to Wales.

The route had now become lush and green; it was pleasant enough before but now there were lots of trees too. We started to get tantalising glimpses of the Wrekin, a famous conical-shaped extinct volcano between Telford and Shrewsbury, while over to the west were the distant Welsh Mountains. I have always found the sight of distant mountains stirring; they suggest an idyllic world amongst them. I will never forget my first sight of the snow-covered

Bavarian Alps as our coach crawled up an unfeasibly long drag on the Autobahn just south of Stuttgart when I was stationed in Germany and off on my first ever-skiing trip.

I was thankful to have company as we entered the very narrow Woodseaves cutting. There was only just enough room for one boat to squeeze through and it was totally blind. It could not have been much fun for the navvies, chopping and shovelling their way through the solid rock, equipped with only hand tools, picks and shovels. After a couple of bends, the five Tyrley locks came into view; there were lots of people around and most of them were willing to help with the locks. I went on ahead with Linda leaving Simon to drive the boat through. The last two locks were quite difficult, once again the canal had taken on a river-like appearance and there was a sign warning potential ship-wreckers to keep to one side. There was another warning to avoid the wash from the gates of the last lock, which was strong enough to push boats away from their course so that you could end up in the trees on the far bank (though this would have caused more inconvenience than disaster). I took over the steering in these last two locks. There was no discussion; we all silently agreed that because the locks were a bit dodgy and it was my boat – if it went pear-shaped, I would only have myself to blame. I was quite surprised to see a huge slab of rock just under the water as *Salamander* slipped by; the various warnings had just mentioned an 'underwater obstruction' and left the details to the imagination (I have subsequently discovered a similar situation just above Trevor near Llangollen but here, the signs just say 'Keep to the middle of the canal' and it is not until you wallop one of the lumps of concrete the size of a small car that you fully appreciate the situation – they really do mean stay in the middle – dead centre!). As Linda opened the gates on the final lock, a huge surge of water attempted to push the boat off course and I did start to drift towards the jungle on my right but a vigorous burst of throttle and some black smoke soon had me back on track and safely into the final lock. There was quite a large collection of 'Gongoozlers' assembled, all looking slightly disappointed that no one had managed to sink a boat today!

We were in Market Drayton at last! I had been looking forward to visiting this market town and tonight I was determined to have a bit of 'culture' – tomorrow was after all my day off again. Tom, another one of my old army muckers, had said Market Drayton was a splendid little town. He had spent some time stationed at Ternhill just up the road, so this would have been the nearest nightlife for him, other than the NAAFI in camp . My only doubt was that Tom was even more cynical than me, so I never knew if his recommendations were genuine or sarcastic. Just like many ex 'airborne warriors' he also seemed to believe that Aldershot was twinned with Las Vegas! Further along the canal. much redevelopment had been going on; there was a smart-looking mooring basin, surrounded by what looked like the usual warehouse conversions. I was not sure who's the berths in this basin were, so I just moored up on the busy towpath. There were narrowboats as far as the eye could see and a sign informing all that mooring was restricted to one night only, making me uneasy as I intended to stay here until Sunday.

Poor old Simon now faced a twelve-mile bike ride back to Gnosall where the van was parked, before returning to collect Linda and driving back to Oswestry where he would no doubt busy himself with a further five hours gardening before darkness fell. I felt a bit guilty again, having nothing more to do than stuff my face, drink tea and entertain Linda until he returned. Normally this exertion would not have bothered Simon in the least, for years he had been a regimental 'racing snake', both runner and cross-country skier but I was a bit concerned as he was still convalescing from serious illness – although you would never know unless he told you this! I said goodbye to my wonderful assistants as they left, they promised to meet me again here on Sunday. After my usual meal of whatever I could fit and cook in one pan, I showered and got ready to go exploring. Because I had done virtually bugger all, I felt unusually fresh, making the prospect of a night out even more appealing.

A sign on the path said 'Town Centre 1/3 mile' and I set off in that direction, through a huge estate of pleasant-looking houses and bungalows. Every few hundred yards, the road changed direction, going alternatively left, then right. then left again with only an occasional sign to reassure me that I was still on course and had not inadvertently wandered into Hampton Court Maze! Twenty minutes later, having walked a good mile, I got to the edge of town. I wondered if maybe the chap that misled me with the phone incident the previous night, was also a town planner for Market Drayton? Handsome black and white half-timbered buildings began to appear here and there, confirming that I was indeed now in Shropshire – a world away from Southeast England.

I went into the first pub I saw – what a dump! Ordering a pint of sanitised lager, I listened to the conversation between the half dozen customers, who seemed to be having a swearing contest with no regard for anyone forced to hear them. This took me back a few decades to when two of my ex-army mates came to visit me while I was still living in Yorkshire. Deano had a monthly routine of staying at my house for the night on his long trek from the Scilly Isles back to the North Sea oilfields. The other character Fred, had coincidentally also arranged to stay on this occasion. He didn't know Deano would be there. They had not seen each other in years, so we kept it a secret which added to the feel-good factor.

The inevitable happened of course, and we headed to the local working men's club. There is a strict code of practice in those northern clubs; some quite rough clientele drink in them but the one thing that is not under any circumstances tolerated, other than a strike-breaker, is swearing (probably rendering about 50% of the customers dumb). To hear Fred talk belied his education and extensive travels – Fred probably single-handedly wrote the army swear manual! On this Monday evening, the place was half full, with only the really serious drinkers in attendance and the three of us propped up the bar. In-between Fred's cockney rhyming slang, every other word started with an 'F' or a 'C'. Deano and I noticed the barmaid's anger and frustration rising but Fred was too engrossed in a story that he was telling us about a Royal Marine who was about to jump from a helicopter when it was relatively still close to the ground, the 'Royal' hesitated for a split second before jumping, by which time the aircraft had climbed to around sixty feet. Whoops! We were both cringing, waiting for the woman to say something (she must have been a Methodist minister in her spare time); she spun around and went absolutely 'rhino', threatening to ban Fred for the next fifty years if he uttered one more profanity. Fred took it all on the chin but looking a little hurt, he turned to us and said;

'What – was I swearing?'

The conversation amongst this bunch of 'chavs', two of whom had their hands wrapped in the inevitable white bandages, took ages to reach a conclusion as people constantly vanished outside for a fag. It seemed to be about some woman who, because of her antics involving drink and drugs, was banned from every watering hole within twenty-six miles of town and the only place she could get a drink now was apparently in Stoke-on-Trent. 'What a shame' I thought, I would have liked to bump into to her later. I made my pint last longer than usual so I could get the full story and then left, hoping not all the pubs here were like this.

Market Drayton isn't the biggest town I have visited and I had soon walked from one end to the other; just to make the natives feel comfortable, there were a token couple of eastern European tramps sitting on some steps, clutching cans of Stella wife-beater lager.

I had read about a pub here that brewed its own beer; I couldn't remember its name but by chance, I happened to wander through its door. there was a plaque on the wall telling us about all the awards their brews had won. I rarely drink real ale now because it usually gives me heartburn for the next four days or thereabouts but tonight I decided to stick my neck out and the stuff was absolutely delightful. I nabbed the last chair in the place and relaxed in the corner happily observing a stream of eager and attractive women coming and going; even the music they were playing was spot on.

I didn't go crazy drinking but I sank enough to ensure a moderate headache would be a certainty next day. I thought the route to get here was complicated but now it was dark and I was a touch the worse for wear. All the streets and houses in the maze I had to retrace through were in total darkness and I had no idea where I was. It was only when someone turned a bedroom light on that I realised that I was in a back garden and nowhere near the road. I ducked down behind the garden shed, trying to think of an excuse if I was challenged. I was starting to feel helpless now, going up one road to find a dead end and then having to retrace my steps only to wander up another identical one.

Finally, I saw a sign pointing to the canal; I cut through another garden then through a gap in a hedge. I stood there for several seconds thinking this is hopeless, I am well and truly lost, when a light flickered from the window of a boat and I realised I was standing on the towpath about a foot from the water's edge. The wave of relief was short-lived as I had no idea where *Salamander* was. I walked right up to the low concrete road bridge on my left, but knew I had not parked the boat anywhere near it, so I turned around and came back the other way until I ran out of boats. Where the hell could it be? I thought about a story I had heard about the Americans allegedly making a battle cruiser invisible during the last war, and then teleporting it five hundred miles – instantly! (Don't tell anyone about this, it is still classified!) I stopped again, scratching my head – and there she was – I felt a wave of relief flow over me and that was the last thing I remembered about the evening.

Just for a change, it was pissing down the next day. I had completely run out of clothes so I would have to do some washing today. There must have been a laundrette in town but for whatever reason, I decided to spend around three hours with my hand-powered pressure washing machine. Yes – a pressure washing machine! My ex-neighbour Martin in Watford had told me about these strange gadgets and I had spent half a day online trying to find one of these nearly extinct machines. When it arrived from Amazon, I spent another half-day assembling it with the usual Chinese-to-English gibberish instructions not helping. When it was built, the thing looked like an old fashion butter churner which is probably where they got the idea from because it worked in exactly the same way, requiring the operator to churn the handle round for hours on end. I have no idea what the pressure element of it did. When I got to the end of this journey, I chucked the thing under the sink and it has lived there ever since, gathering dust just like almost everything else on the boat.

I was still uneasy about the overnight-mooring restriction so I had a quick chat with the people on the next boat. The man told me not to worry about it, he and others often stayed along here for days at a time, adding as I walked away;

'Anyway mate, what are they going to do – clamp your boat?'

I put the DAB radio on to listen to the bullshit and bias news, just in time to hear about some Somalian serial criminal. Someone had decided it would be against the poor chap's human rights to make him wear a tag on his leg. A tag – what about a ball and chain? And I was flapping about staying here a bit longer than I should.

By the time I finished winding the washing the rain had stopped and I thought I would have another look at the town; besides there was no any food left onboard – as usual. I found my way quite easily this time and there ahead was the familiar Asda sign so I ambled over. Just as I got there, a police car pulled up and the 'Plod' got out and grabbed one of the local feral youth, slamming him against the car and making him spread his legs and put his hands on the roof before searching him. I would have liked to stay and watch all this but thought I had better not; it did make me feel quite good though.

Once in the supermarket, I had to doublecheck it wasn't the local jumble sale I had absentmindedly wandered into; everywhere I looked there were heaps of clothes, gardening tools, and cheap-looking fishing tackle strewn on tables in between the food aisles. Strangely, the food items were all neatly arranged on their shelves. I got my bits and pieces and went back to the canal and on the way, I saw three other police cars patrolling the streets. In the space of an hour I had seen more patrolling than I would see in a week back down south. I wasn't sure whether to feel reassured by this, or to take it as warning and buy a stronger lock for the boat door.

It looked as if the rain might stop for more than ten minutes, so I decided to try and dry the washing outside on the clothes-airer. Apart from mad women, I have noticed over the years that I have also become a magnet for insecure, augmentative arseholes and my next visitor reinforced this observation. He walked down the path towards me, then paused and said in a West Midlands accent:

'What yow doin?'

I acknowledged him, saying; 'Well mate, hanging my washing out.'

'Why yow doin it loike that?'

I told the already annoying idiot: 'It's the only way I know of drying my 'dhobi''. He then asked me what the generator was for. I naturally said; 'It's to produce electricity.'

'Woh – I don't need one of those – I can get 220kw from the inverters on my boat.'

He then proceeded to tell me all about his washing machine and I replied that was all very well:

'But you'd be using an awful lot of water doing that, considering that a boat's water tank already needed frequent replenishments.'

He then further bragged that his boat had a thousand-gallon water tank or whatever it was. I muttered under my breath; 'Well you would have, wouldn't you'

'That's not gooin to droy on there.' he continued.

This went on for ages; everything I mentioned, he either contradicted me or out-bragged me. Eventually he changed the subject, asking where I had come from and where I was going. I mentioned Simon and Linda to him, saying they had been a great help; I should have known better.

'Help – wot yow mean loike?'

'Well, if I push you in the canal, then chuck you a life buoy just before you drown, that would be helping you – though I doubt that I would.' I just thought that bit and just managed to restrain myself from saying it. Instead, I mentioned the narrow cutting, saying how difficult it would have been to get through if they had not been with me.

Unbelievably the knob then said: 'What cutting?'

I looked at him, expecting to see a smirk but his face was perfectly serious. I first confirmed that he had arrived here from the same direction as me, I went on now, not caring if I offended him or not.

'Come on mate, don't give me that; there's a mile-long cutting just down there.' pointing my finger in its direction. 'It's cut out of solid rock, you can't really miss it.'

He tried to deny its existence again, saying; 'Nah, I neva cum throw no cutting.'

He must have realised he was beginning to get to me and started talking about Oswestry and all the pubs that stay open illegally until ridiculous hours of the morning, finishing with;

'Well mate, moybay I'll see yer in one of 'em one day.'

To which I replied under my breath; 'Not if I see you first – you utter 'prat'. He was only about five feet tall so I guessed he was probably suffering from 'Small Person Syndrome'!

By early evening I was feeling drained again, not surprising really, with accumulated fatigue and the conversations I had just endured. I have read there are people who live off other people's energy – sort of physic vampires. I had just met one.

So, I had an early night but I shouldn't have bothered – I had another series of mad dreams about the boat travelling under its own command along the canal but at least this time, I confined it to my bed, realising it was just a dream. Another thing I had noticed over the last few days was that my marshmallow-like memory foam mattress had begun to take on the qualities of a slab of concrete! I was developing new aches and pains on a daily basis.

The world's most argumentative man had been right about my washing though, it was still wet. I would just have to hope that any warmth today might get trapped under the cratch cover and dry the clothes. I made my usual pan of porridge, feeling relieved the canal police had not come during the night to drag me off to the tower for staying put an extra night. To be serious, to this day I have never had any problems dealing with the Canal and River Trust; I have always found them reasonable and approachable – so if they could see their way clear to giving me a discount on my next licence – that would be much appreciated, thanks!

It was midsummer's day today, though judging by the temperature and the watery sky, you could have been forgiven for not knowing. Simon and Linda arrived at exactly the time agreed. I felt a bit less concerned now, knowing that each day they helped me, the drive from Oswestry was getting shorter, as we made our way westwards.

While I waited for them to arrive, I watched a shifty-looking character standing just along the towpath making a series of phone calls and looking round anxiously the whole time. His face was black and blue and it looked like someone had extracted their revenge on him; I wondered what misdemeanours he had committed. He wore a pair of those hideous, ubiquitous grey jogging bottoms, baggy at the top and tapering towards the legs. I would love to meet the person who started this fashion trend; why not complete the look with a flashing sign on your head saying; 'DRUG DEALING SCROTE! even if you weren't. I wondered if people turned up for job interviews wearing them?

I had heard about a good ploy to use when cruising under bridges – if any suspicious-looking youths appeared over the parapet who might decide to inflict harm to you or your boat, you should take their photographs, or at least pretend to. As long as the undesirables saw the camera pointed at them it would usually be a sufficient deterrent. I did this now – anything to make his day worse.

Chapter 13

Cheshire and the Border

We were soon underway and cruising through the haunted wooded cutting. The story went that this area was home to a mad (are there sane ones?) screaming ghost who bothered people now and then. I also read there was a much more benign apparition haunting the locks we had come through yesterday at Tyrley, who according to the legend, would help any sole boater mad enough to go through the locks at the dead of night. Once a traveller passed through the gates, the helpful ghost would appear and close them. How thoughtful! I thought – if there were lots more haunted locks, perhaps I could have completed my whole journey in the four or five days the optimistic bullshitters had assured me was possible!

If I were ever abducted by extra-terrestrial beings and dumped back on the towpath without ceremony several years later, naked and confused, I would still be able to recognise within seconds that I was in Cheshire. The rolling green fields were full of dairy cows and in the background was the glorious panorama of the Welsh Mountains, looking very clear and vivid in the distance. In my experience, this meant one thing – rain was on its way (there is a saying about a famous peak in the Yorkshire Dales – *if you can't see it, it's raining. If you can see it, it's going to rain*). To the east there were glimpses of what I thought must be the southern end of the Pennines; Simon pointed out the names of some of the distant mountain ranges. To reinforce the Cheshire theme, a milk tanker trundled alongside a country lane nearby – no grinning cats though!

The stands offering food to the weary traveller became more frequent and we decided to stop and have a look. Linda treated us all to pork pies and some gorgeous lemon drizzle cake. I stuffed it in, thinking that though I was quite an experienced pastry chef, I had never made lemon drizzle cake (though I was pretty sure I could make a decent attempt should the need arise). I also wondered how those lovely people who provided the food, got around the EU Food Safety Regulations. There was nothing I could see to stop a stray cow or giant goose from helping themselves, half eating and contaminating any of the fare on offer. 'Duckshit drizzle cake, anyone?' No one else seemed too concerned though.

So far nothing and no-one had come along to spoil our day and this was how things would continue. There were two series of five locks to get past today, at Adderley and Audlem respectively and I had to check the map frequently because the names sounded so similar. Linda and Simon jumped off the boat walked up to the first lock and sorted things out, enabling me to sail straight in. It may have been Mid-Summer's Day and a Sunday, but there were very few people about, probably due to the weather. By now, we were a well-oiled team and got through the five locks with unbelievable speed. I have noticed since becoming water borne, that when I encounter couples on a boat, more often than not, it seems to be the female who works the locks, toiling away while the men do the really heavy work of leaning back on a rail and steering; usually with a glass of wine in hand. I offered to do my share of the real work but Linda insisted she enjoyed operating the locks and who was I to start an argument? Simon needed the experience anyway. After a respite of only one and a half miles, we arrived at the formidable Audlem flight, a beast with fifteen of the buggers. I said to my wonderful crewmates that I would operate the locks with Linda this time and let Simon do the steering but they had the bit between their teeth now and told me to stay on the boat; they were more than happy to do the tedious job.

Most of the locks here were quite shallow and we got through the first dozen in no time, or so it seemed. Arriving at the well-known, iconic *Shroppie Fly* pub (strange name that, because it's in Cheshire!), I realised why we hadn't seen any other boats or people – they were all here! The pub had originally been a warehouse and it sat right beside the canal. Inside there was a bar shaped like a narrowboat. it was a popular venue and the place was heaving inside and out. There were of course, lots of gongoozlers here.

Simon seemed to know most of them. One of the people he was laughing and joking with looked vaguely familiar; he asked me how I was, and I had the impression I knew him but could not for the life of me remember his name, or where we had met. It turned out this was Chris, who also kept his boat at Chirk Marina and whom I had met the previous New Year's Eve when I had visited. When I met Chris again at Chirk a week or so later, I apologised to him for being so vague. He laughed, saying he realised that I had no idea who he was and that I looked somewhat under pressure that day. I thought that was a bit odd; it had probably been the most relaxing day I had had since starting my little adventure – must have been accumulated stress! We laughed about it, and have been friends ever since.

A family came over to talk to us as we were about to go through the lock next to the pub the young son was fascinated by the sound of the Lister engine so I said I would give him a ride to the next lock, if that was all right. Off we went with an extra passenger for the second time this journey, only this time, we managed to escape any pompous hat wearers!

Once we were through the next three locks, there was a three-mile stretch of rather dreary canal, which looked dead straight though it was, in fact, on a gentle curve. The only thing of interest was a sign directing any invading forces to 'THE SECRET BUNKER.' I commented to my companions that this sounded like something out of an episode of *Monty Python*, or the *Beano* comic but they both just looked at me and grunted. This bunker was built as a sanctuary for the country's leaders, politicians and Des O'Conner, if Armageddon had been unleashed during the cold war era. It was now an eerie underground museum. Simon and I had both served in Germany during this period and there was hardly a day in the seventies and eighties, when we were not reminded we would probably have to fight the Russians one day. It would have been a futile effort though, retreating back to the Rhine and trying to hang on for a few days until reinforcements arrived in the shape of America – that's if we had not already been vaporised by then! We all took this role very seriously (it was not always non-stop beer drinking out there). Looking back, we always seemed to be out in the field, training for this eventuality and every exercise we did had at least a few days in a make-believe Nuclear Biological and Chemical environment. We would quite literally, have to eat, sleep and drink whilst wearing these awful charcoal and paper suits over the top of our normal clothing and just to ensure maximum misery, we would also have to don our respirators, perhaps half a dozen times a day for periods of around of around an hour each time. It was a horrible, near suffocating experience and we hated it. The only good thing was, that in the often freezing German winter, the 'Noddy suit' would keep us warm but in the summer, we roasted. (I only tell you all this to make it perfectly clear that I had, and still have, no intension of ever visiting the well-known 'Secret bunker'.)

We stopped just up from the bunker at bridge number eighty-eight, Baddington Bridge, where Simon could gain road access from the canal. Having cycled all the way back to Market Drayton and picked up his van; he would then return to pick up Linda, and I would continue alone until I found somewhere to spend the night. Simon reappeared about 1 ½ hours later, Linda gathered her knitting and once again we said our good byes. I would have to face the remainder of the voyage alone now until the final day. Simon was always busy, trying to fit a quart into a pint pot (with EU metrication, I wonder if young people today have any idea what this saying means!) but he assured me that when I got to the final leg approaching Chirk, he would come to the rescue again, no matter what. It would be essential not to tackle this alone, that last section was the most treacherous if one did not know the route.

Resuming my journey, I only had to travel another mile before the outskirts of Nantwich appeared; the route took me on an embankment and over an aqueduct around the old salt capital of Britain. There were boats moored on both sides of the canal as far as the eye could see and they took ages to get past, crawling along at tick-over speed, as the many signs implored me to. I had soon learnt that speeding boats (of which there are many) are the biggest cause of raised blood pressure when cruising. The less than pedestrian pace didn't bother me though; it gave me the opportunity to say hello to the many cheerful and smiling faces who appeared to be visiting Nantwich that day. Instantly I thought, forget Wales – this is the place I want to be – and then sailed on straight past it! Eighteen months later, I still have not visited the town. There was no chance of mooring here so I pushed on for a few more miles, almost to Hurleston Junction which is the point where the Llangollen Canal branched off and would be the start of the final leg of my adventure. The canal here was quite wide and could have been mistaken for the Grand Union but there was not much in the way of scenery to inspire along here.

The designated visitor moorings were all taken and the only available place was at the end, so that I had to tie up with half of *Salamander* on the free visitors' section and her other half crossing the permit holder's only part – along with all the associated warnings and consequences. Because of this, I was a lot closer to the next boat than I considered ideal.

My dad used to complain; 'Why is it whenever you go into a nearly empty car park, when you come back, you can guarantee that someone has parked right next to you? It's as if they get lonely!'

He would then go on to tell anyone still listening that he had only ever had one accident in over fifty years of driving when a woman reversed into his stationary car, in of course, an otherwise empty car park!

Later that evening my new neighbour came along to ask me about the generator I was filling with petrol and I took the opportunity to explain why I had parked so close to his boat but he just shrugged his shoulders. We ended up chatting for several hours during which, he gave me lots of information and advice about living on the water. He was originally from Crewe, not a million miles away but like many, after falling out with his wife, he had found himself having to live on a boat. I told him about my decision not to take a different and probably shorter route, via Stone and Stoke and he said immediately I had made the right choice, the route I mentioned would have involved going through the infamous Harecastle Tunnel and he told me about a tragedy that had unfolded there the year before, which made me shudder but I will spare you the details!

As darkness and a cold rain fell, he gave me more advice on how best to get through the four very narrow locks I would face the next day, just around the corner. The secret was to moor the boat to the bollards just before the bridge; the locks were directly beyond and off to the left at 90%. Because of the wash coming from the locks it would be very difficult to moor close to them; I nodded and thought that I understood his advice. The evening ended on a high when he gave me the best part of a full carton of milk, saying he would be gone early the next day. I was not sure how this stopped him from drinking milk but I gratefully accepted it. The subject of my age came up and when I said I was sixty, he told me he was just fifty-one but he thought I looked younger than him – what a splendid chap!

Just like Jay Wynne had predicted the previous night, I was greeted by near gale force winds and horizontal rain – wonderful! The weather was just as bad as on the day I set out from Watford – this really was turning into a summer to remember. Slowly and reluctantly, I put on my boiler suit, fishing suit and one glove – the other having fallen in the water a few days ago. At first it had floated but when I tried to grab it, it sank to the depths in the only part of the UK canal system that is more than three inches deep! Despite the appalling weather I was still not desperate enough to wear the *Dundee* hat but for good measure, I put my old NATO camouflaged windproof smock on top of the layers. I knew that this would confuse everyone I met into thinking that I worked on a building site! I was closer to the junction than I realised and made the exact mistake that my friend warned against the night before. I was not concentrating properly and before I knew it, I had travelled right underneath the bridge I should have stopped short of. When I saw the force of the water gushing from the lock, it made perfect sense; I thought I had understood the situation but this looked like it was going to be interesting.

Immediately around the corner on the left was a line of bollards; I tied the boat up here and climbed up the bank to have a look at the situation. The lock was set against me so I would have to empty it first, adding to the raging torrent already pouring through the not-very-waterproof gates. The lock emptied after around five minutes but the flow of water was just as powerful as when it was full. This really was a strange set-up. Opening the gates ready to enter,

I got back on to *Salamander*, guessing what might happen next. The instant I released the mooring rope, the force of the current together with the howling wind, pushed me backwards across to the right-hand bank so fast that if any other boats had been in the way, it could have caused a nasty collision, but due to the weather there was no other traffic under the bridge, which was now behind me and off to the left. Feeling like a complete idiot, I gave *Salamander* full forward throttle to try and line her up with the lock gates that were now on my left. The boat had not been just pushed backwards, it had also been turned through 90% and I realised that if I had done the correct thing and tackled this nightmare from the other side of the bridge, it would have given me enough time and distance to build up some momentum to push through the torrent – maybe!

Eventually, I got the boat straightened up and headed towards the first lock but just as I was about to enter the chamber, the gates swung closed and I found myself back exactly where I had been a few minutes ago, alongside the bank which had been behind me. I had the usual look round to make sure no one was witnessing this pantomime, or that the host of *You've Been Framed,* was not just about to come walking around the corner with a grinning TV crew.

Pausing for a few seconds, I realised that just when I thought the adventure was almost over, this was the biggest challenge I had faced so far, and that I alone would have to somehow overcome it. This was not just me acting like a plonker, my friendly neighbour of last night had obviously suffered the same problems, or he would not have bothered giving me the advice. I did think it very strange there were no warning signs anywhere.

As I write this I have just looked at the good old *Collins Nicholson Guide*, and they do note that the Llangollen canal tends have a slight flow not dissimilar to the Mississippi and that the bypass weirs can make life difficult. I had missed this; Hurleston Junction is shown twice in different sections but the vital information is only printed on one page – not the one I had seen; I have said already that these books were often difficult to follow. (Incidentally, if you are thinking, how come he has a proper map now, the ancient one I had been given was replaced at some point but I forget where it was – I do however remember buying another *Magnum* at the same time.)

This fiasco happened another three times but on the fourth attempt, I reluctantly gave the gates a push with the boat – and finally I was in – absolutely soaked and having lost most of the feeling in the un-gloved hand. I was halfway out of the first lock when a woman's face appeared to my right; we exchanged Good Mornings, even though it wasn't and I noticed she had a distinct West Country accent.

'Could you close the gate for me please?' I asked.

She immediately frowned and replied; 'No I can't, you cheeky bugger!'

I was taken aback; I said that I thought it had been a reasonable request, considering that she was standing next to it. I was tempted to ask her if she had a right bitch of a daughter living in Rugby and vowed never to visit Devon again, and that she should not expect a Christmas card from me this year! Further along the locks, which were just wide enough to squeeze a narrowboat through with the clearance of a gnat's testicle, I met another woman, this time with a Geordie accent. Just as I was sailing out of the lock she said;

'Har-way pet man, diven't forget tea shut the gate le-ak noow!'

It was beginning to look like it wasn't my day, today. After a very miserable couple of hours, during which time I had also filled the water tank, I was nearly free to continue in the general direction of Whitchurch – and hopefully friendlier people.

It had stopped raining now and the sky had cleared. Before continuing on my way, I looked back to see to a beautiful panorama of lush, green Cheshire countryside stretching for miles below me and I cheered up for a few minutes.

If someone asked me now, eighteen months later, I would say there were no locks between here and Grindley Brook, though in fact, depending where you stop, there are around twelve – but I have hardly any recollection of any of them. I do remember one with a lock keeper who had a white beard and pointed hat and looked like a character out of one of the *Brothers Grimm* fairy tales. He spoke to me in a generic country yokel accent, the one that could belong to anywhere from Cornwall to Norfolk and now apparently Shropshire. I have no idea what he said but I just smiled, raised a hand and carried on. He obviously thought I was fit enough to negotiate the lock unassisted and dashed up and down the canal side muttering, to himself.

I soon arrived at the delightful looking and sounding Wrenbury – and encountered the first of many utterly befuddling lift bridges, which as I was about to learn, are a feature of this canal – and a bloody nuisance! The Wrenbury Mill lift bridge is electrically powered and was fairly straightforward, you just had to keep your finger pressing the button for around a quarter of an hour to raise it and then another similar length of time to put it back where it belonged.

There were four women of around fifty I guessed; all dressed in cycling clothes, and sitting at a picnic table eating their sarnies, their bikes lying on the grass nearby. I said hello and they all replied in American accents. I tied the boat up and went over for a quick chat. One asked me how the bridge operated and I said that was a well-anticipated question because I was about to ask them if they could work it for me. They said they would be delighted to assist me, so after a few instructions, I got back aboard *Salamander* and left them to it.

I asked them where they came from in the USA and they seemed quite pleased that I knew where Maine was. While the bridge was lifting one of them asked me where I was heading and I told her probably Whitchurch. She said they had been there and it was absolutely gorgeous and I should make an effort to visit the town. It seemed a bit odd being urged by an American tourist to go and visit somewhere in my own country! Thanking the cyclists and wishing them well for the rest of their stay, I plodded on.

It was not far to the next bridge. This one was manually operated and just as I got to it, another boat approached from the opposite direction; if we had raced each other, it would probably have been a dead heat. The man on the other boat was also alone and we had a bit of a shouted conversation. It was agreed that I would raise it, allowing him through first, then I would go through and he would lower it – all very civilised and co-operative. The person who designed these bridges must have thought there was a possibility that the odd ninety-three-year-old granny might be required to lift and lower them. The gear ratio was something like one-to-one and cranking them was like riding down a steep slope whilst trying to keep the pedals frantically spinning in the lowest gear available on a mountain bike. There wasn't any resistance at all, taking about 300 revs just to get the thing moving. When the bridge eventually got to the extent of its travel, there was no definite stop point, so you were never quite sure if it was meant to go any higher or not. After ten minutes or so the winch would feel as if the steal cable was about to break and that would be the signal to stop cranking.

The sun was out now and the countryside looked absolutely wonderful. Everything was totally peaceful – that is until I got to Quoisley Bridge. Suddenly a busy road appeared, running absolutely parallel to the canal but slightly higher, so that I expected every speeding car to become airborne and land in the cut. The road sign said the speed limit was forty but most of the drivers were going much faster.

I decided that getting to Whitchurch today was a bit ambitious; there was quite a complex of locks at Grindley Brook, so that would be my limit for today. I had covered just over thirteen miles alone which was not bad, especially after the lock nightmare and the weather. Besides I could dawdle a bit now, if I got too near Chirk I would only have to wait for Simon to pilot me on Thursday.

There was not a great deal to see at Grindley Brook; just the three locks, followed by the well-known staircase locks dominating the scene. I moored just short of the disused Cambrian railway bridge. There were just a few other boats here and everyone I heard seemed to speak with a Liverpool accent. I could not recall buying any food since the visit to Asda last Saturday, which seems a bit strange, as I have explained the need to buy food on a daily basis. Looking back, I can only think that Linda must have brought me some goodies. I certainly didn't buy any food here, all I could find was a canal-side garage shop which did not even sell real food, so I just bought myself another *Magnum* at the usual rural extortion rate.

I had heard stories about long lines of boats waiting to get through the bottleneck caused by the locks here, so after eating my ice cream dinner I felt that an early night was in order. The lock keepers at the staircase started work at eight am and because I was not confident about going through a staircase alone, I would need their support.

The only difference between a normal lock and a staircase apparently, is that a staircase is missing a set of gates! The top gate of one lock becomes the bottom one of the next (or is it the other way around?). This means that boaters must make sure the previous lock is full before starting to ascend as this prevents the embarrassment of running out of water half way up the flight. The other fairly obvious thing is that once started, you have to keep going and cannot stop off for a cup of tea and a sticky bun; it all has to be done in one go. I think the lock keepers' presence was more to speed up the process, thus preventing backlogs all the way to Nantwich or Llangollen, rather than saving boats and crews from having to arrange for very large and expensive cranes to lift them out of bone-dry locks, while dozens of gongoozlers watched and sniggered from the canal side, the rotten sods!

It was not that I was in bed at six o'clock or anything silly but an earlier night than usual seemed a good idea as I was determined to be the first boat there tomorrow. I was up and about well before seven the next day and it actually looked like late June outside. A few people came walking by, coming from the direction that I was heading. we had a bit of a conversation. Just as I was moving off, they confirmed in their scouse accents that as far as they knew, I would be the first boat at the locks – good!

I had heard stories that the lockkeepers here had a tendency to be a bit grumpy and I prepared myself for the worst, but as I approached the staircase one of the keepers saw me and shouted:

'Good morning! Stay on your boat sir and we will see you through.' What could have been more friendly and helpful?

By now I was getting a little complacent after the amount of locks I had operated so far. Standing by the paddles, the 'locky' asked me if I was ready as I bobbed about in the bottom of the first lock and I raised a thumb in the time-honoured way, to confirm that I was. Instantly about 20,000 gallons of water rushed into the lock, slamming *Salamander* and me hard into the bottom gate – for a second I thought the huge heavy wooden gates might come out of their socket and then topple over but, somehow, they withstood the onslaught and we were rocketed up the lock so fast that my ears popped! I half expected to get a severe bollocking from the keepers for not holding the boat steady but they either didn't notice or they weren't that bothered if I destroyed their pride and joy.

This was repeated in the second chamber but this time when the lockkeeper asked if I was ready, I gave the engine some forward thrust to try and counteract the force of the water. Bang – the boat slammed backwards again, with enough force to almost lose my balance and for a second I thought I would to topple into the rapidly filling swirling chasm. I had a little embarrassed look around but there was no reaction from anyone. Waiting for the final rush of water in the third chamber, I gave the engine an even bigger burst of power which of course produced a huge cloud of black smoke, causing a few people walking by to stop and have a look. This time with the engine screaming, I managed to maintain equilibrium and *Salamander* only gave the gate a moderate bump. According to the canal guidebook, these locks only raise the water level by a total of about twenty feet but I have a vivid memory of being surprised and slightly unnerved, not only at the height gained but also by the speed of the accent. The experience had felt like going up in an elevator (or lift as we used to call them, before we were all forced to speak American); I suppose the height gained by the first three locks must have made the rest seem so lofty. Either way, I could see for miles back across the countryside and thought this had been the most exhilarating experience of my journey so far – some people are easily thrilled! I thanked the keepers who had hastened my passage so efficiently and continued on my way for about half a mile.

As I was ahead of schedule, I thought I would go and have a look at Whitchurch, about one and a half miles away. I was starting to feel like it was Ramadan and I really needed to buy some proper food, I could not survive on *Magnums* for another day.

I knew the stub of a disused canal went some, though not all of the way to the town but what I did not know was that just before the spur entrance, there was another lift bridge around a bend and I was almost on it when I saw a boat halfway through and coming towards me. I had to do a sort of emergency stop to avoid a collision but no one else saw this, thinking I had planned it, so that saved a few more of my blushes. Once they knew I was alone, the couple on the approaching boat offered to lower the bridge for me when I was clear. The woman caught sight of my Jerry can with PETROL written on it in white paint (this was a precaution, knowing at some stage I would probably accidentally fill it with Diesel or urine). It lived on the stern deck during the daytime and she was astonished, assuming that I had a petrol-powered boat engine (something I do not think exists – unless you are an early morning whiskey addict – but I could be wrong). After I explained that it was for the 'Genny', I was allowed to go on my way and got going again – for all of 200 yards and that was it – I was almost at the end of the Whitchurch arm!

I could not get the final hundred yards right to the end because the entire canal side was solid with boats but I was lucky, or unlucky enough to find just enough space to squeeze *Salamander* in and after tying her up and locking the door, I set off in the direction of the town. I wasn't entirely sure which route to take, there seemed to be a couple of choices; I went up the hill, past the four ubiquitous, pebble-dashed council houses but my built-in compass wasn't working properly and I ended up going the long way into town.

The four American ladies were right; it was a very attractive-looking place with an ornate clock on a tower in the town centre (I have always thought that towns with fancy clocks in the middle look quaint). Just then a chav drove past in his *Renault Clio* which had been messed about with to look like it had no wheels. The car's exhaust was making lots of farting sounds as he smashed over the speed bumps, going at least twice the speed limit The feral youth had his elbow resting nonchalantly on the window which was of course, fully wound down so everyone else could enjoy the drum and bass noise that was making shop windows vibrate. When he had driven by I looked around to see that there was no number plate on the rear of the car. The old friend who had offered me advice on the futility of arguing with drunks, also once said he believed that legalising bare knuckle boxing was a viable solution to a lot of today's anti-social problems; I tended to agree.

After going around in yet another circle, I was back exactly where I had been five minutes earlier, next to the big clock. I really could have done without the exercise today; everything hurt, from my ear lobes down to my neck, back, hips and feet. I walked over to the bus station where I had seen signs for Tesco but I just couldn't find it.

Like the Gnosall incident, my usual method when lost is to take up the challenge and just keep walking until I find the place that I am looking for -. I have had a few arguments with women friends over the years, unable to grasp my logic (or eccentricity) and seeming to me to give up far too easily, making no attempt to walk miles but simply asking the first person they saw for directions – surely that's cheating! However, I was ravenous by now, and half the morning had already gone, so, spying a studenty looking lad, I politely asked him if he knew where Tesco was. He started laughing and pointed across the road.

'It's just there, you can't really miss it.'

He was right too. He said he was also going there and walked over with me.

I told him about my journey and he said: 'Wow cool!' I said 'Uhm, yeah' under my breath.

The day was sweltering now and I managed to find yet another route back to the canal, up a steep hill via a park complete with bandstand. Once I had stowed the shopping and had a couple of mugs of tea, I got the engine going. Hopefully things would feel cooler once I got moving.

There was a winding hole at the very end of the stub where I would have to turn *Salamander* round before I could continue the voyage. At first it looked big enough to spin a super tanker around in, though things can be deceptive! I untied the boat and started to reverse her across the pond, feeling relaxed and confident that there was plenty of space – followed by that sinking feeling – no, there wasn't enough room – the winding hole had suddenly shrunk. I put the boat into forward gear; if I went forwards then chose a different angle, maybe that would do it. Reversing again, the space seemed to get even less. I went forward again; the front of the boat hit the canal side but when I tried to go back again, I had run out of space here too. I had about six inches of space behind me and about the same at the front. Faffing around for ages, to-ing and fro-ing I was achieving nothing. The boat ended up trapped, the front and rear were both now touching their respective sides of the canal. It was as if *Salamander* had somehow grown by another ten feet and the space available was just getting less and less before my eyes! Of course, people were stopping now and annoying me more by muttering and tutting to each other. An angry looking man of about my age, who looked a bit like Norman Wisdom, appeared. I have been wary of Norman Wisdom look-alikes ever since I had a Company Sergeant Major who bore more than a passing resemblance to the comic. I pointed this out to the lads once, causing much nodding and sniggering. It was only an appearance mind; the CSM was the complete opposite of the real Norman, angry, impatient and aggressive. Soldiers are bigger gossips than the average fishwife and it was only a matter of time before my jibe got back to him and he could persecute me even more.

This Shropshire Norman started to pace up and down like an expectant father, shaking his head. The way he was behaving, I thought maybe he owned the canal.

Still pacing, he began to shout: 'No! No! No!' over and over. I had no idea what he was so offended about. He was shouting something else now.

I stopped revving the engine so I could hear properly and yelled, 'What?'

'You can't turn that there!'

I shouted back, 'Why not? It says it's a winding hole on the map.'

I had pronounced *wine-ding* wrongly of course again, making him even angrier. He had another bout of 'No. No. No-ing!' I just could not understand why he was taking it all so personally. I had another go at wriggling out of the impossible space; deaf to his new rant, then stopped revving again.

'I can't hear you!' I shouted.

As the engine noise died down, the man shook his head once more, and stormed off towards the direction from whence he had first come to bother me. Suddenly he about turned and came back but now he was much calmer, saying 'Throw me the bow rope!'

I scrambled my way to the front, ready to oblige. We could talk now in a more civil manner and he asked me how long the boat was.

'Fifty-four feet I told him.

'That's too long for this hole mate.'

'Oh, I see, I thought it said seventy feet on the map.'

'No, no, no ...' he started off again.

'What?' I said.

In the end, he fastened the rope to one of the bollards as a pivot, while I gunned the engine, together with lots of rudder movement. Slowly and much to my relief, the boat swung around and was facing the right direction. The gathered crowds started to disperse, Norman amongst them.

I just managed to shout; 'Thanks very much!' to him.

I heard later that the story made the headlines in the local rag the following week! What a palaver for nothing! On reflection, I should have just left the boat at Grindley Brook and walked the mile or so to town.

And just to make things worse – in all the excitement of looking at fancy clocks and doing my numerous circuits of the town – I had completely forgotten to get some money from the cash machine! There was no way I was going to stagger back through the now near Saharan heat, I would just have to manage without any money until I got to the next civilisation at Ellesmere, that wouldn't be today though.

There were now lots of Welsh looking black-and-white half-timbered houses popping up everywhere, along with bi-lingual signs. Apparently, these were there just in case you had forgotten that 'Slow'! was English for 'Araf'! as you slid off a hairpin bend and plunged into a rocky ravine! For the rest of the afternoon, I barely knew which country I was in. I was in good company though; multiple factions have been arguing for centuries about where the ever-moving border was. When we came this way by car, en-route to our holidays in Pembrokeshire years ago, I thought in my seven-year-old imagination, that these half-timbered buildings were exclusively occupied by witches, probably from seeing pictures of Welsh ladies wearing national dress, with tall black hats. On one journey, the weather was awful and we stopped off at a tearoom in a '*Hansel and Gretel*' like cottage. My parents were having a whispered conversation and I got really anxious that we would have to stay the night here, the old hag who served us was more than a little witch-like in appearance. In reality, the whispering was probably just about the price of the scones.

I had managed to waste a good half of the day with my little excursion and it was just as well I was not in a hurry now because it was well into the afternoon. After passing a boat yard located right underneath a huge and busy concrete road bridge, I arrived at the next lift bridge.

The mechanism to operate it was on the far side of the bridge and on the opposite side from the towpath. My heart sank as I tried to work out what to do. I stood on the stern for a minute, looking and scratching my head while *Salamander* started to wander about. The real problem was that the usually solid canal sides had gone and instead, a muddy reed-infested swamp surrounded the bridge. If I raised the bridge, there would be no way I could get back to the boat.

I was stumped and suddenly regretted leaving my fishing waders in the garden shed that I had bought with my neighbours, back in Watford. (They never did offer me a refund when I left). Suddenly the cavalry turned up in the shape of another boat with a couple on board. I didn't need to say anything, they immediately offered to help me to get through, which they did.

Once we were both clear I really had no choice other than to follow them, uttering repeated appreciation and apologies at the other impossible-to-negotiate-alone bridges, which were all identical. After the third, I deliberately dropped behind them a bit. I know it is in the nature of canals that boats do tend to follow one another but I was quite blatantly depending on their goodwill to get through every bridge and I began to feel like a canal-borne stalker. Of course, it would have been absolutely no skin off their noses to help me; they had to go through the bridge anyway but I still felt uncomfortable. What really bothered me was they had an aloof air about them, not unlike my nemesis with the lock wars a few weeks before. I had tried making small talk with them, when we closed up at the bridges but they had made it quite clear they did not wish to talk to me. Perhaps they were worried I might invite myself for dinner later and then guzzle all their wine, or maybe they only had a couple of evenings to get it 'on' during a secret 'business' trip!

I began to feel more relaxed once they disappeared into the distance, apart from wondering how I was going to get through the remaining bridges. As it turned out, there was only one more to get under that day and checking my diary, I have made no comment, so it must have been plain sailing.

I was now going over a dead straight stretch of canal on an embankment; this was Wixall Moss, a peat bog. The guidebook as usual, made the area sound as if it was on a par with the Egyptian pyramids or the Grand Canyon but the pretty rolling scenery had gone and was replaced by a boring, featureless landscape. It reminded me of the bleak and barren live firing ranges at Tidworth on Salisbury Plain. I was impatient to get beyond it all.

Smack bang in the middle of all this was the junction for the Prees Canal branch – the canal to nowhere! This stretch had been restored just to keep lift bridge freaks entertained – there were two of them in the space of less than a mile and unless you were going to the marina at the end, you would have to turn around and come back again through the same bridges you went under ten minutes earlier – pointless. I had no inclination ever to explore it!

After forty or so minutes of tedious cruising, I reached the end of this modern-day wonder and the canal began to twist and turn again and the scenery became pretty once more. Just to complete the scene, the sun blazed and there was not a cloud in the sky. I had bought a bit more food than usual in Whitchurch so it did not matter where I stopped tonight. Not much further on I saw a pleasant and secluded spot with not another boat to be seen; this would do me for the night. It was a good choice too; after the usual fiddle with the now decapitated TV aerial which had come to grief as I went under one of the numerous rabbit-hole-sized bridges, I threw it back on the roof in disgust and looked at my road atlas instead for entertainment.

The aerial became damaged some time ago which was my fault, not realising a theodolite would be needed to keep

Salamander absolutely dead centre of the bridges which of course, the builders had placed on a series of hairpin bends. I knew what was about to happen as I watched the aluminium pole snap like a carrot when it contacted the 180-year old stonework. I stood watching but just managed to catch it before it pinged off the side of the bridge and fell into the canal. Miraculously it still worked – but not where I was now. Looking at the remoteness of the area, I wondered if they were still using dial-up Internet and gas lighting. Once I had showered and felt human again, I went and stood perfectly still on the towpath and just listened; apart from some cows mooing in a field about three miles away, there was not a sound. I have rarely known such tranquillity; it was bliss. The nearest hamlet to here was Welshhampton – which of course is in England!

The only thing that disturbed me that evening was a working boat going by which wasn't really any hardship. The skipper could not possibly have gone by any slower and when he got level with me, I said the usual good evening stuff and thanked him for his consideration, commenting that it was a shame more people didn't slow down properly when passing moored boats. He said it was no problem, and something about 'do unto others'. The woman at the rear of the boat, picked up on my comments, saying loudly in the broadest of welsh accents;

'Yeah, not like the idiot behind us who has been tailgating us all afternoon – the bastard.'

She said this loud enough to make sure the offender was left in no doubt about her sentiments towards him! Once again, I remember little about the rest of that evening, except that I slept for ten hours that night...again!

Chapter 14

Light at the End of the Tunnels

This was the penultimate day then and I wasn't quite sure how to play it, Ellesmere was only just up the road, not really far enough to call it a reasonable day's cruising. On the other hand, Chirk was too far to get to in one day. Besides, as I have already stated, the last section up to Chirk was particularly tricky to attempt alone and Simon had been adamant that I should not try to dock the boat in the marina on my own and I took his word for it. So, for now at least, it seemed I had all the time in the world. I had only travelled a couple of miles before I saw an inviting looking spot with trees everywhere forming a green canopy over the water; rays of sunlight filtered through the leaves making the place look enchanting and there were some black and white half-timbered buildings opposite, no doubt occupied by witches! I stopped and got a brew on the go, then sat at conveniently placed picnic table enjoying the solitude and the warm sun. This was the third fine day in succession, maybe summer had finally arrived,

People who think they know me are often surprised to find out that I meditate most days. I do this twice a day, for twenty minutes at a time. Whether it provides any lasting benefit, I am not sure, but what I do know is that when I am doing my best to think about nothing other than my breathing, I often experience delightful sensations although they usually fade the moment I allow my mind to take control again and the endless internal thought processes start once more. When I had finished my tea, I closed my eyes and began the ritual and opened them twenty minutes later, just in time to see a boat going silently by with the occupants staring at me open mouthed, no doubt wondering if I was all right. They probably thought I was trying to cope with some huge hangover, seeing me sitting upright, unmoving with my eyes closed.

Batteries recharged, I continued on to Ellesmere but I had completely overlooked the piddling eighty-seven-yard tunnel that lay ahead. I soon woke up though, when *Salamander's* bow hit something at the tunnel entry and ran aground, half in half out. The boat stopped and then moved to the left at an awkward angle and I was just thinking I would have to go to up front and sort things out when a family emerged from the darkness, walking towards me. They saw immediately what had happened; three of them gave the boat a pull and I was free again to carry on. The remainder of the journey into the town was flanked by one lake or mere as they are called in this area, after another, with sparkling water, greenery and sunlight everywhere. The scene looked stunning.

Ellesmere is one of the most important centres on the Llangollen canal; I had expected it to be busy and it was, there were boats moored all over. I grabbed a space just before a bridge, almost opposite the marina and after the usual security procedures, I set off to walk into town. I had been here briefly last year with Simon, when he had taken me on a whistle-stop tour of possible mooring places in Shropshire and North Wales. I wandered through the narrow quaint streets trying to remember where I had seen Tesco some six months previously. When I eventually did find it, it was right next to the canal and I realised that once again, I had taken the scenic route. I didn't mind the extra walking this time, I was in chill mode at last and could take my time.

I let my mind have a little – what if? – wonder. I had seen a job advertised in Ellesmere a few years earlier. I met all the requirements of the post (I was already doing an almost identical job), so I decided to apply for it. However, I did not get the application form until Friday and the closing date was the following Tuesday.

It was a Bank Holiday weekend and I realised there would not be time for my application to arrive by post. I called the person mentioned in the advertisement and though she sounded a bit surprised – after a bit of humming and hah-ing – she told me to send the application back by fax which I did, sending the completed form to Shropshire on the Sunday afternoon, I never heard another thing about it. Nothing unusual about that I suppose but I suspected that the short list for interviews had already, unofficially taken place just before the holiday weekend and my surprise last minute application might had been conveniently deleted by the person I had spoken to, when she came into work on the Tuesday morning! Or it could have been genuinely forgotten about and not discovered until after the deadline when it would have suffered the same fate, thus avoiding any questions or embarrassment. Whatever became of that application, I cannot help thinking today that Ellesmere would have been a great place to live and work.

I eventually arrived back at the boat, hot and sweaty, carrying two bulging Tesco bags in one hand, leaving the other free to tackle the inevitable *Magnum* I was attempting to eat before it was turned into a milkshake by the hot sun. The thought occurred to me, that maybe I was getting a bit addicted to these calorie-laden treats – they would be stopped the moment I reached my final destination!

There was a huge sweeping bend to my left with a signpost pointing to Llangollen and among other sundry notices around, one warned of unfeasibly shallow waters, saying the canal was not suitable for boats over 2' 6" draft. I knew what this meant but had no idea what *Salamander's* draft was, though I remembered having to invent some figure when I was taking out insurance for the boat. As the original, owners of the boat had apparently travelled the seven seas in her and there was every likelihood that they too, had ventured up this neck of the woods once, I decided to take the risk. Another disturbing sign warned reckless idiots that the bridges were a bit tight too. I wondered just how small they could be, considering I had already knocked everything possible off the roof on what were presumably, normal sized bridges; the only thing left unscathed by now was the paint.

The huge sweeping bend was not quite as huge as it first appeared and I had to reverse and make a second attempt, providing great amusement to a gentleman who looked rather like a drunken version of the 1970's TV character, *Catweasel*. He was sitting in what looked like a land-based fisherman's coracle which surprised me because the only photos I had seen of these strange boats were on fast flowing rivers in Mid Wales, not on Shropshire canal tow paths.

Leaving my hirsute friend to his drunken rambling I got on with navigating the now snake-like route; there wasn't a moment to relax. The advertised tight bridges were situated of course always on a bend, and they now appeared every few hundred yards. There was absolutely no way of knowing what might be lurking around the next blind corner and to make things more interesting, the wind had also strengthened again.

The inevitable happened on one particularly tight bend; as I emerged from under a bridge another boat was coming towards me, only feet away. As I panicked, putting *Salamander* into neutral and immediately losing any steering, a well-timed gust of wind slammed her midships into the side of the other boat. The skipper had a shocked expression on his face which was hardly surprising and as we got level, I apologised profusely, saying to him, how sorry I was. My main concern was that just before impact, I had seen a woman sitting in the cratch area, totally unaware of what was about to happen – the poor woman was just sitting there minding her own business knitting – then suddenly wallop! I said I hoped his wife was all right, expecting a bit of a lecture but he just said very magnanimously;

'It's alright, it's nothing that we haven't all done at some point!'

I just replied with; 'Oh – alright then.'

On later reflection, I think we were both equally to blame; I just hope his missus didn't drop a stitch in the impact; having to explain to relatives that the Christmas socks were a funny shape because they had originally started life as a scarf!

Every time I let the boat drift slightly off centre, I got a sharp reminder as she lurched violently, struggling to get free of the rocky bottom. At times it felt like I was on a fair ground waltzer and I was starting to take the depth warnings seriously now. The lack of water underneath made worse by the now, very pronounced flow from west to east. *Salamander* almost came to a complete stop at every bridge and I thought if things got much worse, I would have to start dismounting at all the bridges and pushing her, thinking a mule would have been useful.

At last the non-stop twisting and turning began to ease and the canal became straighter. I slid past Lower Frankton locks that guard the entrance to the Montgomery Canal – another waterway to nowhere! This is a bit unfair; the canal does go to places like Pant, Welshpool and one day to Newtown. The problem is that there are several gaps in it – which would spoil your plans if you wanted to actually go anywhere. Despite the discontinuity, it is still very popular. So much so, that passages have to be pre-booked on it. I thought it would be nice to live long enough and be in good enough health to be able to sail all the way to Welshpool one day. I have since walked along a section of this canal, where contractors and volunteer workers are doing a splendid job of restoration.

Going under a low road bridge, suddenly the canal became dead straight with a long line of hire boats moored by some buildings. This was Maeststermyn, or as I like to say when I feel like deliberately confusing people, 'Monstermunch', another place I had visited previously, on New Year's Day. I decided this was where I would spend the final night of my long journey. There was a pub on the bridge just behind me and that would do nicely.

I didn't like the look of the 440kw power cables that hung across the canal from huge pylons, hissing menacingly. But surprisingly, when I tried the PC TV plug-in and did the nightly tuning ritual, I got one of the best receptions I had found so far. Not that it mattered, I would be spending most of the evening in the pub. I called Simon to let him know where I was and he sounded surprised I had made such good progress from where they had left me two days ago. He and Linda decided to come and visit me that night and keep me company in the pub; it would be a short drive for them now as Oswestry was only a few miles away. I still had no idea if I was in Wales or England; the nearest real village from here was Welsh Frankton but don't be fooled by the title – it means nothing!

I put my jacket on and made my way along the towpath towards the road bridge a few hundred yards away. Stepping off the path onto a dead straight main road, for a second I could have been back down south again. There was no footpath and the only way across the bridge to the pub was by walking along a 9" strip of dusty margin, separated from the road by a white line. I hoped I could do it without wobbling too much which would have meant certain death, as the constant stream of cars thundered past at 98mph. I was quite concerned that I would have to do the same thing again later as it would be dark by then and I would probably be a bit the worse for wear too.

When I eventually got to the imaginatively named *Narrowboat,* I was shaking a bit but Simon and Linda had arrived already and made themselves comfortable in a corner. They were surrounded by old office equipment – computers, printers, fax machines and dial-up modems which had just been unceremoniously dumped there. These were presumably to relieve the boredom, something to look at while you ate your 'Hunter's Chicken' and drank your beer. (I have subsequently decided that Hunter's chicken must be the official 'national' dish of Shropshire, and most of North Wales).

The scene behind the bar was even more entertaining; there were only two staff, a young woman of about twenty who was desperately trying to keep her cool with her colleague, who I estimated to be about ninety-four! It was taking him around ten minutes to pour out a half pint of beer and I think he must have been in charge the cooking too – there were twenty or so very hungry looking customers, all sitting together at the far end of what looked like a railway waiting room, leaving us three at the other end. After an hour or so and a couple of pints or glasses of red wine, my company said goodnight, agreeing to meet me here (well not in the pub) the next day at about nine. I had another pint alone and thought I had better call it a night, knowing that I still had the perils of the bridge to face. Fortunately, the traffic had quietened down a bit as I stepped into the darkness. I waited for a gap in the speeding traffic and made a dash for it, shaking slightly as I got to the safety of the path down to the canal and wondering how many people must have been killed walking along that bridge drunk, over the years. I could *Google* it later!

When I left the boat earlier to walk to the pub, I had been the only one there but now there was a long line of nose-to-tail (or should that be bow-to-stern?) boats crammed together just in case they got lonely. I decided there was no point in worrying about the close proximity of neighbours; I was half-cut and knackered and would soon be fast asleep, despite those angry high-tension power cables dangling above the boat's roof.

I had to study the canal guide a few times to get a clear image of the remainder of the route – as I have said, I found these books quite confusing and in the age of Satnav, I wondered how the navigationally challenged boater would cope – some of them might never have seen a real map. (I have probably just answered my own question; they use a *Garman* device and do not worry too much about wrong turning or one-way streets.) Initially my confusion had led me to believe we would be crossing the world-famous viaduct at Pontcysyllte but a more careful reading showed me this feature was two miles beyond Chirk, and would not therefore, form part of today's journey.

I was still sorting things out inside when Simon and Linda arrived and the next thing I knew, the engine was running and we were underway. I was treated to the novel experience of seeing the countryside pass by from the inside of the boat. I think at that moment I got it – to be able to enjoy the sight of places slipping by from the comfort of your own surroundings was great – providing you trust the person driving, which of course, I did.

I joined my friends on deck: the countryside was achingly beautiful now, further enhanced by the glorious weather. The canal however, became more tortured than ever; twice

I had to grab the exhaust pipe when it looked likely to hit the top of the stonework under the ridiculously low bridges, it was always potluck going under them, especially as there always seemed to be a turn involved just waiting to throw the boat off her centre line. If this was not enough to contend with, the water was getting busy with hire boats and their usually clueless crews, lurking around just about every bend. The terrain here is hardly flat but there are only two locks on this entire stretch of canal, at New Marton; the canal builders having planned the route to avoid the worst of any inclines. Arriving at these two locks, there was quite a bit of activity; one couple in a boat coming towards us got a bit excited when I started operating the paddle gear and it was a while before they realised that I was doing this to help them. As we got under way again, I noticed a large plume of steam rising above the surrounding hills and remembered the huge wood-products factory at Chirk; a bit further on we could smell the place too.

Canal-side houses and cottages began to appear now, hugging the canal, and lots of the gardens came right down to the water. I could imagine visitors from Japan seeing this and almost wetting themselves with excitement, I would not have blamed them either, it all looked so enchanting. Going under the busy A5 road, we took a few more turns and suddenly we were going over the massive stone-built Chirk aqueduct. The railway viaduct carrying the old Great Western Line from Shrewsbury to Chester and beyond, ran parallel to it and once upon a time, it would have been possible to take a train from Birkenhead to London Paddington, without changing seats or tickets. Just as we got to the middle of the aqueduct, a train slid by (I say train; it was really just a couple of buses converted to run on rails.) and I went into daydream mode. This scene reminded me of a painting in a book I was given for Christmas when I was about six. It was a fantasy panorama scene, with a proper steam train going over a massive bridge; under the bridge was an ocean-going liner and in the sky above was a huge propeller-driven aircraft. Also going under the bridge was a canal, complete with narrowboat. The picture also showed road traffic and anything else that would have been around in the 1960's, or at least, in the imagination of the artist. The caption read, 'Which mode of transport would you choose?' At six or seven, to me that would have been a no-brainer – train!

I was thinking that this scenario was probably the closest thing in the real world to that painting The company name was written on the sides of the two coaches; *Arriva Trains Wales*. It has crossed my mind a few times recently – how could one company have the monopoly to run every bus service in the country as well as most of the trains – now apparently – who are they and how come no one has noticed? I could bet that one thing is for sure; they are not a British company. Did you know that Deutsche Bahn, formerly the German state railway, owns Chiltern Railways?

Just to add to the surrealistic situation, a tunnel mouth now loomed at the end of the aqueduct – I have to admit that Chirk tunnel took me completely by surprise, I had completely missed it on the map – I was now having a momentary overload with so much to take in!

Simon suddenly said; 'You will have to get off and have a look.'

The tunnel entrance was situated on a curve with no way of seeing if there anything was coming the other way.

I jumped off and tied the boat to the nearby bollards: the tunnel was clear after all but as a precaution, I took the exhaust pipe off. After checking the headlight was on, we vanished into the gloom; Linda sensibly went and sat at the front of the boat in comfort and safety. This was a horrible little tunnel (well they all are!), particularly because there was a very noticeable current, making it feel as though we were standing still. We must have been breathing almost pure diesel exhaust too now that the pipe had been taken off. The tunnel was only four hundred yards long but I was glad to see the last of it as we emerged into the deep cutting that now surrounded us. Up above the right-hand bank I could see that we were now going right past the hideous *Kronospan* factory. It spewed out its constant God-knows-what into the surrounding countryside and of course – just as at the other factories I had passed – there was not a soul to be seen.

Chapter 15

The Arrival

That was it then – another half mile and I saw the canal-side signs advertising all the services on offer at the Chirk marina. Simon swung *Salamander* off to the left on the very tight route into the marina proper. After three weeks of travelling, 210 miles, 255 locks, and fifteen *Magnum Classic* ice creams, you might expect that I would now be in very good spirits – I had made it to my destination – albeit after a few dramas and setbacks. But all I felt now was a huge sense of anti-climax and an increasing feeling of foreboding. Maybe I had expected the local brass band turning out to welcome my arrival!

Simon went into the office to ask where I should put the boat and once he was back on board, we carefully threaded our way through the dozens of other boats moored everywhere.

I was a bit surprised when Simon said to me; 'What you should do now is nothing; just relax and do nothing for two weeks.'

I was fairly exhausted after this journey and thought to myself if Simon is saying that, then maybe I do need a rest. (It was short lived – after only one day of the good life, someone came knocking on my door asking if I fancied a bit of work – but that is a completely different story!)

The whole journey was almost in vain – the first day in Chirk something disturbing happened. As usual I needed to go shopping and as usual, I did not have a clue where the village or town was (a tip for anyone thinking of visiting Chirk – it is nowhere near the marina – the only thing they have in common is the name). I went into the café/bar in the marina and asked the woman behind the counter where I could find a shop. She gave me directions but gave me the impression she did not really know. I set off following her vague directions but after walking for around half an hour, up and down a couple of vicious hills, I was almost level with the 'chemical weapons factory' again.

I decided I was going the wrong way; my surroundings were getting very rural and I could not imagine finding a shop along here. I turned around and retraced my steps, past the marina and on to the main road. After a four mile walk in the blazing sun, I finally got to Chirk and got the few things I needed. I noticed that the girl serving me added twelve pounds extra on to the total; there had been some misunderstanding and to give her the benefit of doubt she was not deliberately trying to rip me off but still, this was hardly a welcoming gesture. Continuing my walk, I have never in my life been stared at so much, I was half expecting every car that drove past me to crash into a wall. Maybe walking is some sort of taboo activity in Wales, I thought; surely they can't all know each other so well that they can instantly spot an intruder? It was very strange.

This was not the disturbing thing though: the footpath in Chirk constantly changes from one side of the road to the other and anyone mad enough to attempt walking has to wait every few hundred yards for the endless traffic to stop so they can get to the other side – only to repeat the entire pointless madness again just up the road. Maybe that is why they were all staring?

It was during one of these path-changing crossovers that it happened – I stopped and looked right, then left. A car was coming towards me but it was a few hundred yards away and travelling at, or below the 30mph speed limit – or so I estimated. I glanced once more to my right and stepped into the road. There was a very long, loud blast of a car's horn and I stopped instantly. The same car I had seen seconds ago, was about three feet away from hitting me. It is hard to convey the shock and fear I was feeling; how the hell could this be possible? There was no swearing or the usual hand gestures from either of us. The only good thing was that I got to see the expression on the young driver's face. He looked just as shocked as I felt.

I walked back to the boat slowly and carefully. 'Just think Martin – one more step and the last three weeks would have been entirely pointless.' I wonder if the canal trip would have got a mention at the funeral and if so, would the guests present have appreciated the dark humour?

There was another twist to all this; I had mentioned the car incident to a local lad that I worked with and several months later, over a few pints the story came up again but this time my workmate turned to me and said;

'Oh yeah, that was my younger brother that almost ran you down; he admits he was speeding, and off his head on dope too!'

WHAT! I was more shocked now than when it happened. I started to say; 'Tell your little scrote of a brot –' but then thought there was really no point.

When I tell people about the long cruise from Watford, they often ask me if I would do it again. To which I reply;

'Yes, but only if I could walk it.'

When the comedian Jo Brand did her now famous *Across the Pennines Walk*, she covered 135 miles in seven days. At that speed, she would have completed my trip in just twelve days. I had taken twenty-three days to cover the distance (I took three days off from the torment and was actually travelling for nineteen days), that is nearly half Jo's walking speed!

Exactly a week after arriving in Chirk, Simon picked me up early on a blistering hot first of July, the hottest day we had seen over the last two summers, to drive me back to Watford so I could collect my car. It was very strange arriving back where I had started after only a couple of hours of driving. We even crossed the same canals in various places which made the experience even stranger. I sat outside the office in the marina drinking a coffee, telling a few people about the last few weeks. One of the optimistic bull-shitters walked over and said:

'How far you got then?'

I told him I had got the whole way and I was now about to drive back to be reunited with my boat. I could see he was a bit ruffled to hear that I had succeeded and asked me how long it had taken.

When I said three weeks, he scoffed. 'Nah, I would have dan that in four days!'

I knew I would probably never see the irritant again and quickly came back with;

'Sod off mate, you reckon could cover over thirty miles per day – alone? Bollocks!'

He was determined to have the last word though; 'Oh well, maybe six days then!'

People are usually astonished when I tell them I still have no interest in boating – probably less now than before I embarked on the long ride up here. However, I must admit, I have weakened somewhat and have been out three times since arriving here; with a CRT licence costing around £900, that works out nicely at £300 per trip! Once last summer, I went to the nearby Lion Keys Spa (in the pouring rain of course) and felt quite disappointed on finding that there were no actual lions roaming the grounds. What they have got is an annoying peacock that screamed all night, ensuring that sleep was impossible. I thought at first it was someone being murdered, until I saw the bastard hanging from the top of a fire escape and decided enough was enough; I would go back to Chirk at first light. It was some consolation knowing that the guests staying in the overpriced rooms at their companies' expense, would have got no peace either.

I have also taken *Salamander* up to the delightful Llangollen a couple of times. The run up there is particularly hazardous alone through the numerous narrow, blind channels but I have done it – and have lived to tell the tale. Of course, going to 'Llan' as the locals call it, involves the nerve-shattering crossing of the aforementioned World Heritage Site, Pontcysyllte Aqueduct – 126 feet above the River Dee – which is really spectacular. The secret of getting across the aqueduct is to not bother steering, just let the boat do its own thing in its trough, it is quite safe – you will not go off the unguarded side! While I have been writing this book, I have started to think that if I write a sequel, I suppose I will have to venture out on another voyage – We will see.

Once things had settled down I found myself against the odds, sweltering away again in a commercial kitchen but the employment was on a flimsy basis and by the following January, it had dwindled to nothing. As I have said, I hoped to pursue my performing arts in this neck of the woods and had managed to do a number of days the previous summer. Now without a job, I would be able to concentrate on my magic more and planned to get out there as much as possible during the tourist season. The following summer, I performed on numerous occasions in various towns nearby and Llangollen proved to be my favourite venue. Although a bit commercialised, 'Llan' is a charming town with its numerous black and white ancient buildings and the surrounding mountains.

One morning, while I was doing my thing, I was joined by a group of Jehovah Witness recruiters, who although friendly enough, it was obvious that what they were attempting to sell was not entirely compatible with my own wares. Pointing this out to the 'happy clappers', I offered to move to a more favourable position on the steps outside the tourist office. One of them replied that they had been removed from there on a previous occasion. I said nothing but felt quite privileged, knowing that I was always tolerated in the town where, apparently magic was favoured over religion, even if they are based on the same thing fundamentally!

These magic outings have been fitted in around the numerous days and weekends when I wasn't busy assisting Simon, either teaching survival training to youngsters or cooking corned beef hash on an authentic vintage field stove, to be offered free to the bemused public as part of a World

War 1 presentation (this subject is Simon's passion). This year the diary is already full with lots of dates, enough to keep us both busy throughout the summer months. I never imagined that in my sixties I would still be playing with fire and slashing my fingers on jaggered corn beef tins – There must surely be scope for someone to invent a user-friendly twenty-first century tin can!

Another great bonus is that I have rekindled my interest in painting after rather losing interest for a number of years. This renewed vigour is almost certainly due to being surrounded constantly by the stunning scenery in this area. So, remember, if you see a dodgy-looking bloke performing magic or selling paintings in the street – say hello and give me a generous tip. You probably would not recognise me though unless I am ordering fish and chips – I am usually smiling when busking!

Finally, I did look into the drunken death statistics for Maeststermyn Bridge and there aren't any – so apparently, no-one in the last forty years or so has wondered into the path of a speeding vehicle there. Arriva Trains Wales, is really Arriva Trains from Germany! *Branston Pickle* it turns out, comes from a village called, not surprisingly, Branston in Staffordshire – although I still prefer my version of its origins!